504

4-12

Reptiles & Amphibians
of the West

Vinson Brown

ILLUSTRATED BY Carol Lyness
AND Phyllis Thompson

NATUREGRAPH PUBLISHERS

Library of Congress Cataloging in Publication Data

Brown, Vinson, 1912—
　　Reptiles and Amphibians of the West.

Bibliography: p.
　　1. Reptiles — The West.　2.　Amphibians — The West.
I. Title

QL653.W4B76　　　　　　598.1'0978　　　　　74-3204

ISBN 0-87961-029-8 Cloth Edition
ISBN 0-87961-028-X Paper Edition

Naturegraph Publishers Inc., Healdsburg, California 95448

TABLE OF CONTENTS

LIST OF ILLUSTRATIONS

Reprinted by courtesy of Little, Brown and Company, from
How To Make A Miniature Zoo, by Vinson Brown, illustrated by
Don Greame Kelley.

Color Plates

Black and White Plates

HOW TO USE THIS BOOK

This book is a simple and brief introduction to the reptiles and amphibians of the West. Watch and learn about these interesting creatures and their fascinating habits rather than destroy or hurt them, because civilization is already killing off more of these creatures than can reproduce themselves in many localities. Unless you are an actual scientist or studying to be a scientist and need to make a scientific collection, it would be much better for you to study and observe these creatures at a distance, or photograph them, or, at most, capture them alive for short periods so you can watch them in aquariums or terrariums. After a few weeks of this, they should be let loose into their natural habitats in the wild. Remember that in some states, however, it is unlawful to collect certain reptiles, even for a zoo, without a special permit. Find out the rules of your state before doing such collecting.

In studying animals in the field it is wise to have a pair of field glasses or a small telescope so you can observe them from a distance without disturbing them. Move very slowly and quietly and stay still for long periods of time. Look each kind up in this book when you have observed it and taken sufficient notes to help you in identification. Especially watch for prominent markings, colors and distinctive shapes, but also note the habitats or living places where each creature is seen and how it acts. If you go out at night take a flashlight with a powerful beam, preferably one you can carry on your head or hat, and shine it wherever you hear noises. Approach very carefully and quietly until you can get the animal in the beam. Two people going out together with lights can do better, as they can locate a noise, such as a frog's call, by turning the lights toward the sound from two different angles. Where the lights cross the animal is likely to be. Patience and trial and error will make you expert at this. Use the *Key to Shapes* shown on pages 10-13 to decide what type of amphibian or reptile you have seen, then turn to the proper pages of the book to look it up, or simply thumb through and look at the pictures. It will help you in doing this to mark with a special symbol each animal in the book that is found in the neighborhood where you live or are visiting. When you visit any new region make a new special mark for all animals found in that region. Then you will not waste time looking at pictures or descriptions of animals that are not found where you are located.

How to collect, cage and care for live amphibians and reptiles is briefly described on pages 6-9. Under each species description, or group of species, information is given on what these animals prefer to eat. This will help you if you keep animals temporarily in captivity.

In each species description, the size is given first, then the geographic range and the habitats in which each animal is found, next the color and peculiarities of shape, and last, when not described in the family or order description, the food habits. While most reptiles and amphibians described in this book are quite distinctive, others may look very much alike. In this case the geographic locality, habitats and habits of two such similar species should be studied carefully, for these often are different.

HOW TO CATCH REPTILES AND AMPHIBIANS

Many pet stores have various reptiles and amphibians for sale, or can obtain them for you, and will also furnish you, in most cases, with food you can give them. If you wish and have the opportunity to collect your own live specimens, however, the following are some suggestions that will be of help to you.

Some species are so rare or hide so well by day that they are hard to find. A knowledge of the habitats in which they live (given in the accounts of the species) and by using methods of hunting by night (see page 5) are of use in finding them. The more secretive animals should be looked for especially in and under objects on the ground such as logs, rocks, boards, piles of debris and so forth. Turn over these things and look under and through them, but *please remember to turn everything back in place after you are through so that animals can find shelter there in the future.* Usually, when a log or rock is turned over, the animal under it is momentarily shocked into stillness, and this is the instant to seize it. In the West only the rattlesnakes, the Coral Snake and the Gila Monster, among reptiles or amphibians, can give you a poisonous bite, so study the descriptions and pictures of these and learn where they are found so that you can avoid picking them up by mistake. Otherwise, all other reptiles and amphibians in the West are perfectly safe to handle, though a few of the larger species may bite you hard enough to give some temporary pain. Large snakes and lizards are best seized behind the head on the neck so they cannot turn and bite. Both reptiles and amphibians can be placed in cloth sacks, such as that shown on page 7, but amphibians need to have a fair supply of damp moss or something equivalent put in with them to keep them from drying out while you carry them home. It is generally best to carry amphibians home in a small jar with damp earth and leaves on the bottom.

To catch a lizard out in the open it is often wise to use a loop on the end of a long thin stick (as shown on page 7). A fishing pole is very good for this, as it can be telescoped out quickly to a long, thin length. Don't make the cord to your noose too long, as it does have a tendency to wave in a breeze. Gently and slowly approach the lizard until you can slip the noose over its head and jerk it tight. You can also set traps for these animals (as shown on page 7). A still more effective can trap is made by carefully balancing a tin lid attached to a wire that stretches across the top of the can so an animal stepping on the lid will fall into the trap. The wire screen trap shown can be left out at night and investigated in the morning. To make it still more effective, use eight inch high or more boards or wire mesh on either side to form a V-shaped double fence line from twenty feet or more out leading the animal right to the trap's mouth. The barrel trap for turtles is easily made by sinking the barrel in a pond near a natural swimming place for turtles, holding it in place with stakes and arranging a ramp with bait on the end that will be so balanced that when a turtle reaches for the meat it will fall into the barrel. *Be sure to visit all traps daily!*

You can also collect turtles and amphibians in ponds with the net shown at the top of page 7. The net and hand screen shown should have about quarter inch wide mesh so that the water will move through each easily when swept through the water.

6

Use the dip net in quiet water

→ current

Use the hand screen in swift streams

Collecting bag

Can trap sunk
in the ground

Wire screen or hardware cloth
concealed in bushes

← Ramp: any handy material

Tools & traps for reptile collecting

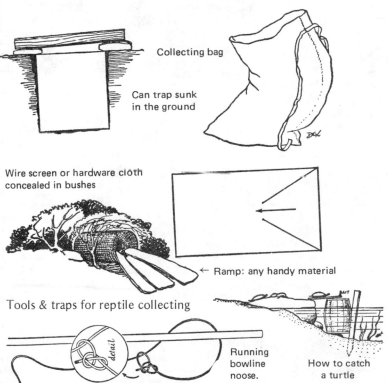

Running
bowline
noose.

How to catch
a turtle

detail

Courtesy credit on illustration page.

7

TAKING CARE OF REPTILES AND AMPHIBIANS IN CAPTIVITY

Terrariums, which are ideal for taking care of most reptiles and amphibians, may be obtained at any pet store. Try to arrange each terrarium in your home zoo in such a way as to duplicate as closely as possible the original habitat from which a group of animals came. Thus animals found in a woodland would be put into a terrarium with dark humus soil put on a coarser base soil and.in which plants and rocks are arranged attractively to copy the original woodland appearance (see page 9). For a pond-side habitat, in which frogs, toads and salamanders can comfortably live, produce a pond at one end of the terrarium and higher ground at the other end, using soil and plants commonly found in a pond-side habitat. Clean the waste matter of the animals out of the terrarium at least once every two days, and be sure that any water is kept thoroughly clean. In a desert habitat terrarium you would use a sandy soil and some gravel in which are planted desert plants. In cold weather it is wise to keep a small light burning over the terrarium so your animals always stay warm. Be sure to use a stainless-steel terrarium, not a painted one that might rust or poison your pet.

In the summer time it may be a good idea to dig a pit in your backyard (with a roof if you have a rainy summer), put in cement walls if possible (though a hard vertical clay-dirt wall may do), and have an island in the center on which plants or a plant for shade is growing. Lizards and snakes find this natural place attractive for living, and can be easily watched by visitors. In such a pit keep a pan of clean fresh water at all times. Various cages can be bought at pet stores that will also hold lizards or snakes, and these cages are best if they have bases that are waterproof and can easily be cleaned.

Treat every animal with the utmost kindness, as they also suffer, even as you do, from lack of food or water, or too much or too little dryness or humidity. With frogs and salamanders it is usually best to keep a glass top about a quarter inch above the sides of the terrarium to keep in the moisture. Desert reptiles, of course, need little moisture. Let animals go free when you become tired of them.

In the species accounts of the following pages the preferred food of each kind of animal is usually given. Your pet store can often furnish live meal worms with which to feed the lizards, amphibians and snakes. Very young animals, especially among the amphibians, can be fed by collecting leaf mold from a wood or park, putting it in a funnel inserted in a jar, on the bottom of which has been placed some damp blotting paper (see page 9). The heat of a light placed above will drive the tiny worms and insects of the leaf mold down onto the blotter from which they can be easily taken to feed the animals.

Some snakes need frogs or pollywogs, others prefer mice or rats. Numbers of white mice can be raised in captivity for this purpose, and can often be secured cheaply from pet stores, or a nearby college. Some snakes can be fed by gently forcing small pieces of raw meat down the throat with light taps of a slender blunt stick, but be very careful not to push too hard and puncture the flesh.

8

HOMEMADE CAGES, PITS AND TERRARIUMS

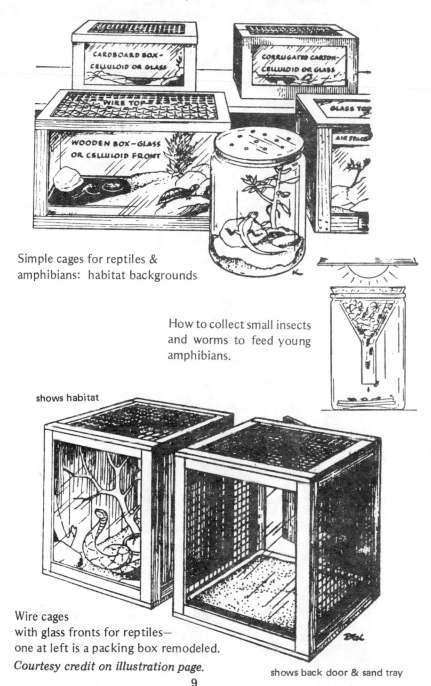

Simple cages for reptiles & amphibians: habitat backgrounds

How to collect small insects and worms to feed young amphibians.

shows habitat

Wire cages
with glass fronts for reptiles—
one at left is a packing box remodeled.
Courtesy credit on illustration page.

shows back door & sand tray

9

KEY TO REPTILES AND AMPHIBIANS BY SHAPE

AMPHIBIANS

Warts all over body. Hind legs long. *Toads.* p p. 21, 23-24 and 54-57.

Hind legs long, but no warts on body. *Frogs.* p.p. 23-26 and 54-55.

Hind legs not extra long, and tail found in adults. *Salamanders.* p p.17-20 and 50-53.

REPTILES

Body snake-like, but has moveable eyelids, and tail breaks off easily. *Legless Lizards.* p p. 58-59.

Large shell on back, *Turtles & Tortoises.*

Scales on belly are large, quadrangular and arranged in eight longitudinal rows; head with distinctive shape. *Whiptail or Racerunner Lizards.* p p. 35-37.

Strong fold of skin between belly and back. *Alligator Lizards.* pp. 34-36.

Eye with pupil vertical. *Night Lizards* pp. 62, 63, 65; *Geckos* pp. 58-59.

Eye with pupil round. Most *Lizards.*

Even, quadrangular scales on belly; head flat on top. *Night Lizards.* pp. 62-63, 65.

10

Rather tough scales on back; legs moderately strong. *Iguanid Lizards.* (Some unusual Iguanid Lizards are shown on right.) Iguanid Lizards usually have different kinds of scales than are shown on this page. p p. 28-33 and p p. 61-63.

Iguanid Lizard with markedly fat stomach. *Chuckwallá.* pp. 58,61.

Back and head with granular or bead-like scales. *Gila Monster.* p p. 58-59.

Iguanid Lizards with horns on body and head. *Horned Lizards.* pp. 60-61, 63.

Iguanid Lizard without ear opening. *Earless Lizard.* p p. 27-28.

Small granular scales on top of head. *Geckos.* p p. 58-59.

Toes with side-scales. *Leaf toed Gecko.* p p. 58-59.

Base of tail constricted; skin very soft. Typical *Geckos* of genus Coleonyx. p p. 58-59.

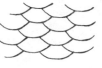

Back scales smooth, overlapping, shaped like meat-choppers; tail of young often blue. *Skinks.* p p. 33-34.

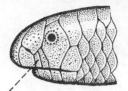

Small, almost useless eyes; belly scales same shape as back scales. *Blind Snakes.* p p. 64-65.

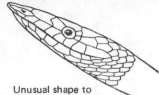

Unusual shape to head of Colubrid. *Vine Snake.* p p. 66-67.

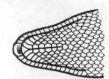

Scales under chin of same general small size. *Boas.* p p. 64-65.

Large scales or chin shields under chin. p p. 38-48 and 66-73.

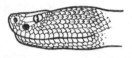

Heat-testing pit between nostril and eye. Rattle on tail. *Rattlesnakes.* p p. 46-48 and 70-73.

Typical Colubrid or common snake head; also found in *Coral Snake.* p p. 38-46 and 66-71.

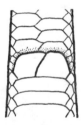

Two rows of scales under tail in most Colubrids; anal scale divided.

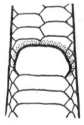

Two rows of scales under tail in Colubrids, but anal scale single. *Glossy, Garter, Gopher and King Snakes.* pp. 43-48; 68-70.

Anal scale single, but scales under tail in only 1 row. *Longnosed Snake.* pp.38, 40.

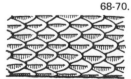

Keels down middle of back scales in Colubrids. *Garter, Gopher, Rough Green, Hognose, Lined, Water, Corn and Rat Snakes.*

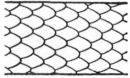

Scales on back without keels in rest of Colubrids.

12

CHECK-LIST OF SPECIES

ORDER, FAMILY AND COMMON NAME

Because this book has been produced so as to cover a great deal of information in a small space, and because we have put the most colorful species in the color plates side, by side thus showing similar looking species together, the arrangement of species and genera in this book is not based on their scientific relationship. However; this proper relationship by order and family is given below for your convenience in understanding where each species belongs in nature's arrangement. The number of each species in the book is given for quick reference to the generic and specific names and to the descriptions. A few species are so rare in our area that they are listed here and described briefly on pages 15 and 16.

CLASS AMPHIBIA

Order CAUDATA

Family AMBYSTOMIDAE
- ☐ Long-toed Salamander (9)
- ☐ Northwestern Salamander (10)
- ☐ Olympic Salamander (11)
- ☐ Pacific Giant Salamander (7)
- ☐ Tiger Salamander (8)

Family SALAMANDRIDAE
- ☐ California Newt (12)
- ☐ Red-bellied Newt (14)
- ☐ Rough-skinned Newt (13)

Family PLETHODONTIDAE
- ☐ Arboreal Salamander (1)
- ☐ Black Salamander (2)
- ☐ California Slender Salamander (4)
- ☐ Clouded Salamander (3)
- ☐ Del Norte Salamander (112)
- ☐ Dunn's Salamander (111)
- ☐ Ensatina (108)
- ☐ Jemez Mountains Salamander (115)
- ☐ Larch Mountain Salamander
- ☐ Limestone Salamander
- ☐ Mount Lyell Salamander (109)
- ☐ Oregon Slender Salamander (6)
- ☐ Pacific Slender Salamander (5)
- ☐ Sacramento Mountain Salamander (116)
- ☐ Shasta Salamander (110)
- ☐ Siskiyou Mountain Salamander
- ☐ Van Dyke's Salamander (113)
- ☐ Western Red-backed Salamander (114)

Order SALIENTIA

Family ASCAPHIDAE
- ☐ Tailed Frog (32)

Family LEPTODACTYLIDAE
- ☐ Barking Frog (117)

Family PELOBATIDAE
- ☐ Couch's Spadefoot (18)
- ☐ Great Basin Spadefoot (17)
- ☐ Plains Spadefoot (15)
- ☐ Western Spadefoot (16)

Family BUFONIDAE
- ☐ Colorado River Toad (128)
- ☐ Dakota Toad (124)
- ☐ Great Plains Toad (123)
- ☐ Green Toad (19)
- ☐ Red-spotted Toad (127)
- ☐ Sonoran Green Toad
- ☐ Southwestern Toad (126)
- ☐ Texas Toad
- ☐ Western Toad (121)
- ☐ Woodhouse's Toad (125)
- ☐ Yosemite Toad (122)

Family HYLIDAE
- ☐ Arizona Treefrog (22)
- ☐ Burrowing Treefrog
- ☐ California Treefrog (23)
- ☐ Canyon Treefrog (21)
- ☐ Chorus Frog (24)
- ☐ Cricket Frog (25)
- ☐ Pacific Treefrog (20)

Family RANIDAE
- ☐ Bullfrog (26)
- ☐ Cascades Frog (118)
- ☐ Foothill Yellow-legged Frog (30)
- ☐ Green Frog
- ☐ Leopard Frog (28)
- ☐ Mountain Yellow-legged Frog
- ☐ Red-legged Frog (31)
- ☐ Spotted Frog (29)
- ☐ Tarahumara Frog (119)
- ☐ Wood Frog (27)

Family MICROHYLIDAE
- [ ] Great Plains Narrow-mouthed Toad (120)

CLASS REPTILIA

Order TESTUDINATA
Family CHELYDRIDAE
- [ ] Cooter
- [ ] Desert Tortoise 179)
- [ ] Painted Turtle (104)
- [ ] Pond Slider (106)
- [ ] Snapping Turtle (177)
- [ ] Sonora Mud Turtle (178)
- [ ] Western Box Turtle (103)
- [ ] Western Pond Turtle (105)
- [ ] Yellow Mud Turtle (102)

Family TRIONYCHIDAE
- [ ] Smooth Softshell Turtle
- [ ] Spiny Softshell (107)

Order SQUAMATA
Family GEKKONIDAE
- [ ] Banded Gecko (130)
- [ ] Leaf-toed Gecko (129)
- [ ] Texas Banded Gecko (131)

Family IGUANIDAE
- [ ] Banded Rock Lizard (49)
- [ ] Bunch Grass Lizard (44)
- [ ] Chuckwalla (134)
- [ ] Clark's Spiny Lizard (39)
- [ ] Coachella Valley Fringe-toed Lizard (143)
- [ ] Coast Horned Lizard (138)
- [ ] Collared Lizard (36)
- [ ] Colorado Desert Fringe-toed Lizard (142)
- [ ] Crevice Spiny Lizard (41)
- [ ] Desert Horned Lizard (140)
- [ ] Desert Iguana (38)
- [ ] Desert Spiny Lizard (40)
- [ ] Eastern Fence Lizard (46)
- [ ] Flat-tailed Horned Lizard (141)
- [ ] Granite Spiny Lizard (43)
- [ ] Greater Earless Lizard (34)
- [ ] Leopard Lizard (37)
- [ ] Lesser Earless Lizard (35)
- [ ] Long-tailed Brush Lizard (50)
- [ ] Mojave Fringe-toed Lizard (144)
- [ ] Regal Horned Lizard (139)
- [ ] Round-tailed Horned Lizard (137)
- [ ] Sagebrush Lizard (48)
- [ ] Short-horned Lizard (136)
- [ ] Side-blotched Lizard (52)
- [ ] Small-scaled Lizard
- [ ] Striped Plateau Lizard (47)

- [ ] Texas Horned Lizard (135)
- [ ] Tree Lizard (51)
- [ ] Western Fence Lizard (45)
- [ ] Yarrow's Spiny Lizard (42)
- [ ] Zebra-tailed Lizard (33)

Family XANTUSIIDAE
- [ ] Arizona Night Lizard (146)
- [ ] Desert Night Lizard (145)
- [ ] Granite Night Lizard (147)
- [ ] Island Night Lizard (148)

Family SCINCIDAE
- [ ] Gilbert's Skink (53)
- [ ] Great Plains Skink (55)
- [ ] Many-lined Skink (56)
- [ ] Mountain Skink (57)
- [ ] Western Skink (54)

Family TEIIDAE
- [ ] Checkered Whiptail (63)
- [ ] Chihuahua Whiptail (66)
- [ ] Desert-grassland Whiptail
- [ ] Giant Spotted Whiptail (67)
- [ ] Little Striped Whiptail (70)
- [ ] New Mexican Whiptail (64)
- [ ] Orange-throated Whiptail (61)
- [ ] Plateau Whiptail (68)
- [ ] Six-lined Racerunner (69)
- [ ] Texas Spotted Whiptail (65)
- [ ] Western Whiptail (62)

Family ANGUIDAE
- [ ] Arizona Alligator Lizard (60)
- [ ] Northern Alligator Lizard (59)
- [ ] Panamint Alligator Lizard
- [ ] Southern Alligator Lizard (58)

Family ANNIELLIDAE
- [ ] California Legless Lizard (132)

Family HELODERMATIDAE
- [ ] Gila Monster (133)

Family LEPTOTYPHLOPIDAE
- [ ] Texas Blind Snake (150)
- [ ] Western Blind Snake (149)

Family BOIDAE
- [ ] Rosy Boa (151)
- [ ] Rubber Boa (152)

Family COLUBRIDAE
- [ ] Banded Sand Snake (164)
- [ ] Black-necked Garter Snake (168)
- [ ] California Lyre Snake (160)

Family COLUBRIDAE (cont)

☐ California Mountain Kingsnake (91)
☐ Checkered Garter Snake (83)
☐ Coachwhip (78)
☐ Common Garter Snake (86)
☐ Common Kingsnake (89)
☐ Common Water Snake (165)
☐ Corn Snake (95)
☐ Desert Hook-nosed Snake
☐ Glossy Snake (96)
☐ Gopher Snake (97)
☐ Green Rat Snake
☐ Ground Snake
☐ Huachuca Black-headed Snake
☐ Lined Snake
☐ Long-nosed Snake (71)
☐ Mexican Garter Snake (169)
☐ Milk Snake (88)
☐ Mountain Patch-nosed Snake (158)
☐ Narrow-headed Garter Snake (167)
☐ Northwestern Garter Snake (87)
☐ Plain-bellied Water Snake (82)
☐ Plains Black-headed Snake (72)
☐ Plains Garter Snake
☐ Racer (77)
☐ Ringneck Snake (74)
☐ Rough Green Snake
☐ Saddled Leaf-nosed Snake (156)
☐ Sharp-tailed Snake (75)
☐ Smooth Green Snake (76)
☐ Sonora Lyre Snake (161)
☐ Sonora Mountain Kingsnake (90)
☐ Sonora Shovel-nosed Snake (93)
☐ Sonora Whipsnake (81)

☐ Spotted Leaf-nosed Snake (155)
☐ Spotted Night Snake (162)
☐ Striped Racer (79)
☐ Striped Whipsnake (80)
☐ Texas Lyre Snake
☐ Trans-Pecos Rat Snake
☐ Vine Snake (159)
☐ Western Aquatic Garter Snake (84)
☐ Western Black-headed Snake (73)
☐ Western Ground Snake (163)
☐ Western Hognose Snake (153)
☐ Western Hook-nosed Snake (154)
☐ Western Patch-nosed Snake (157)
☐ Western Ribbon Snake (166)
☐ Western Shovel-nosed Snake (92)
☐ Western Terrestrial Garter Snake (85)

Family ELAPIDAE
☐ Arizona Coral Snake (94)

Family VIPERIDAE
☐ Black-tailed Rattlesnake (171)
☐ Massasauga (98)
☐ Mojave Rattlesnake (170)
☐ Red Diamond Rattlesnake (100)
☐ Ridge-nosed Rattlesnake (173)
☐ Rock Rattlesnake (175)
☐ Speckled Rattlesnake (172)
☐ Sidewinder (176)
☐ Tiger Rattlesnake (174)
☐ Twin-spotted Rattlesnake
☐ Western Diamondback Rattlesnake (101)
☐ Western Rattlesnake (99)

SOME RARE SPECIES

The following species are not often seen by the average person in the area covered by this book, though some are fairly numerous elsewhere, such as in Mexico or further east. If an unusual specimen is found that does not seem to fit the descriptions given in the bulk of this book, turn to this section and see if it fits the species described here. The numbers given to each species in this list tie in with the species number nearest it in appearance in the regular part of the book.

AMPHIBIANS

Larch Mountain Salamander, *Plethodon larselli*. Lower Columbia River gorge, usually under bark or rocks or in rotting wood. Distinctive reddish undersides. (113)
Siskiyou Mountain Salamander, *Plethodon stormi*. Northwest California and Southwest California, generally found among broken rock piles. Similar to Del Norte Salamander (112), but dark back frequently finely-speckled yellowish or whitish; also back stripe rather rare.

SOME RARE SPECIES

Limestone Salamander, *Hydromantes brunus*. Lower Merced River Canyon and Bear Creek, Mariposa Co., California. In crevices of limestone cliffs and the broken rocks below, liking moss-covered rocks. Similar to Mt. Lyell Salamander, but with uniform white or yellow on belly and brown on back and head. (110)

Texas Toad, *Bufo speciosus*. West Texas and south New Mexico, often burrowing among mesquite or in grasslands; breeding in still water. No back stripe, evenly warty. (123)

Sonoran Green Toad, *Bufo retiformis*. South central Arizona, night living in grass under mesquite and in creosote desert. Network of black lines on back. (19)

Burrowing Treefrog, *Pternohyla fodiens*. South central Arizona, burrowing in grasslands under mesquite bushes. Distinctive helmet-shaped head. (21)

Mountain Yellow-legged Frog, *Rana muscosa*. In higher California Sierras. Similar to Foothill Yellow-legged Frog, but with dark toe tips and usually more spotted. (30)

Green Frog, *Rana clamitans*. Southwest British Columbia and northwest Washington, in ponds and streams. Similar to Bullfrog, but has folds of skin along sides of back.

REPTILES

Cooter, *Chrysemys concinna*. West Texas and southeast New Mexico, mainly in rivers. Similar to Pond Slider (106), but has brown or black circles on back.

Smooth Softshell Turtle, *Trionyx muticus*. Eastern New Mexico and north Texas, in rivers and lakes. Similar to Spiny Softshell (107), but has smooth front to carapace.

Small-scaled Lizard, *Urosaurus microscutatus*. Resembles Tree Lizard, but found in entirely different area, mainly in eastern San Diego Co., and south into Baja California. (51)

Desert-grassland Whiptail, *Cnemidophorus uniparens*. Southeast Arizona and Southwest New Mexico, and south into Mexico. Only whiptail with olive-green to greenish-blue tail and a striped yellow and brown back. (70)

Panamint Alligator Lizard, *Gerrhonotus panamintinus*. Found only in Panamint, Inyo and Nelson Mountains in California. Sharply dark-banded on back and tail. (58)

Rough Green Snake, *Opheodrys aestivus*. Central and east Texas, climb in trees and bushes in damp woodlands. Similar to (76) but scales rough.

Trans-Pecos Rat Snake, *Elaphe subocularis*. Southeast New Mexico, west Texas and south into Mexico, in dry areas. Pale brownish with long H-shaped black marks on back. (95)

Green Rat Snake, *Elaphe triaspis*. Southeast Arizona and south. Plain greenish or olive snake, unmarked on belly. (95)

Plains Garter Snake, *Thamnophis radix*. Southern Alberta, eastern Montana, Wyoming and Colorado, and southeastern New Mexico. Bright orange or yellow stripe on back and bright yellow belly. (83)

Lined Snake, *Tropidoclonion lineatum*. Eastern Colorado and northeast New Mexico; looks like striped garter snake, but has 2 rows of black spots on belly. (166)

Ground Snake, *Sonora episcopa*. Eastern New Mexico, west and central Texas. Similar to (163), but more often dark-blotched on back and head.

Desert Hook-nosed Snake, *Ficimia quadrangularis*. Southeast border of Arizona and south into Mexico. Similar to 154, but with saddle-like black markings on back.

Huachuca Black-headed Snake, *Tantilla wilcoxi*. Southeast border of Arizona and south into Mexico. Broad white neck-band; black cap curves down to corner of mouth. (72)

Texas Lyre Snake, *Trimorphodon vilkinsoni*. Southern New Mexico and far west Texas and south into Mexico. Similar to 161, but lyre-shaped marks on head fainter.

Twin-spotted Rattlesnake, *Crotalus pricei*. Southeast Arizona and south into Mexico. Only rattlesnake with 2 rows of black spots down back. (170)

16

AMPHIBIANS

Class Amphibia—Amphibians—Feed mainly on insects and worms. (See also pages 50-57.)

The Class Amphibia includes the salamanders, frogs and toads, all of which are characterized by a moist skin that feels soft to the touch and by the fact that most of them go through a metamorphosis, changing from the egg into legless larvae (pollywogs) and then into adults with legs. While the salamanders have even-sized legs, the frogs and toads have the hind legs developed for jumping. Adult salamanders keep their tails, but frogs and toads lose the tails they had in the larval stage. Most amphibians spend at least part of their life in water, and, during the water stage, generally have gills, which in adulthood change to lungs. Some have developped strong land-living habits (see below).

Order Caudata—Salamanders. (See also pages 50-53.)

Salamanders, which also include the newts and water dogs, are not as regularly involved in complete metamorphosis, as are the frogs and toads. Some have, in the adult stage, neither gills nor lungs, but breathe through the skin. Some salamanders, which are permanently aquatic, develop only gills. Some salamanders lay their eggs not in water but in damp places on land and complete the larval stage within the egg. (Lengths given are those of adults.)

LUNGLESS SALAMANDERS

Family Plethodontidae—Lungless Salamanders. (See pages 50-53.)

1.   ARBOREAL SALAMANDER, *Aneides lugubris*. 2½ to 3 7/8" from nose to tail-base. Found from Humboldt County, California, south, mainly in coastal ranges, to the northwest corner of Baja California. Most are associated with live oak trees, but some are found in the Sierra foothills opposite the lower San Joaquin Valley in the Digger and Yellow Pines and Black Oaks. *Powerful jaws show bulges at sides of head;* color as shown, but spots vary greatly in number, size and position.

2.   BLACK SALAMANDER, *Aneides flavipunctatus*. 2½ to 3" from nose to base of tail. Found from the Mt. Shasta region west to coast north of Eureka, California, and south in coast ranges to San Francisco Bay, in fairly open coniferous forests. An isolated subspecies is found in Santa Clara and Santa Cruz County mountains, with fewer spots and flecks. Color of individuals as shown in two pictures, with more all black forms found also in far north of range; *undersides dark slate or black.*

3.   CLOUDED SALAMANDER, *Aneides ferreus*. 2¼ to 2¾" from nose to base of tail. Found from Mendocino County, California, north in coast ranges to central Oregon coast, then inland through Willamette Valley and base of the Cascade Mountains to the Columbia River. An isolated subspecies is on Vancouver Island. Likes open coniferous forests and climbs trees even more than does Arboreal Salamander, being often found under bark, etc. Color as shown, but sometimes dark brown colors predominate; *dark gray to dark brown belly usually speckled with white, or may be all white.*

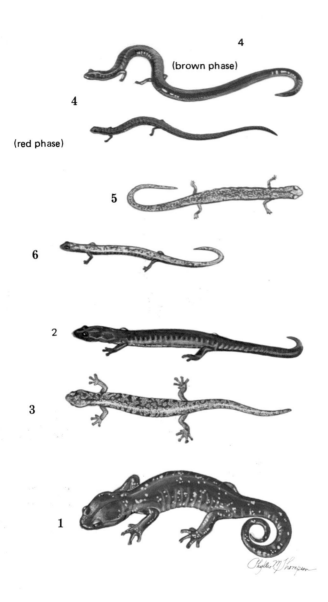

4

(brown phase)

4

(red phase)

5

6

2

3

1

1. Arboreal Salamander
2. Black Salamander
3. Clouded Salamander
4. California Slender Salamander
5. Pacific Slender Salamander
6. Oregon Slender Salamander

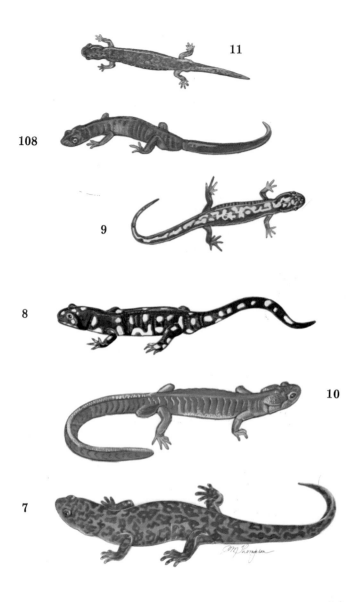

11

108

9

8

10

7

7. Pacific Giant Salamander
8. Tiger Salamander
9. Long-toed Salamander
10. Northwestern Salamander
    108. Ensatina Salamander
11. Olympic Salamander

4.   CALIFORNIA SLENDER SALAMANDER, *Batrachoseps attenuatus.* 1¼ to 2" from nose to base of tail. Found from southwest corner of Oregon south along California coast and main part of Great Central Valley and central Sierra foothills to northern Baja California. All slender salamanders have 4 toes on each foot, one quite small. *This species uniformly colored brown or red; very tiny legs.* Often wriggles violently when disturbed.

5.   PACIFIC SLENDER SALAMANDER, *Batrachoseps pacificus.* 1½ to 2½". In foothills and mountains of Los Angeles area. *More dark brown than above.*

6.   OREGON SLENDER SALAMANDER, *Batrachoseps wrighti.* 1¼ to 1¾". Found in northern Cascade Mountains of Oregon in coniferous forests under bark and debris. *Distinguished by large white blotches on black belly.*

LUNGLESS AND AMBYSTOMID SALAMANDERS

108.   ENSATINA SALAMANDER, *Ensatina eschscholtzi.*   (See also pages 50-51.) 1½ to 3" long from nose to tail-base.

Family Ambystomidae—Ambystomid Salamanders.

7.   PACIFIC GIANT SALAMANDER, *Dicamptodon ensatus.* 4½ to 6½" from nose to tail-base. Found from extreme southwest corner of British Columbia south through western Washington and Oregon to northwestern California, inland to Lassen Peak region, and south to Monterey Bay. Likes humid forests, generally in water or under bark, rocks, etc. *Has large size and striking mottlings or marblings on back and head.* Gives both rattling and sharp, barking cry. Feeds not only on insects, but also on shellfish, crayfish, small snakes and mice.

8.   TIGER SALAMANDER, *Ambystoma tigrinum.* 3¼ to 6" from nose to tail-base. Found as an isolated population in central California west of the Sierras; also east of a line that extends from south central British Columbia and the northern edge of central Oregon, south through central Idaho, western Utah, northern and southeastern Arizona into northeast Mexico. Likes mammal holes, crevices and holes in logs or stumps during dry weather, going near water when it rains. *Distinctive blotches or spots of yellow, yellowish-white or grayish above;* unusual head shape; grayish or pinkish on belly, with soft yellow marks.

9.   LONG-TOED SALAMANDER, *Ambystoma macrodactylum.* 2 to 3¼" from nose to tail-base. Found from northwestern British Columbia and southeast corner of Alaska south and east to southwest Alberta, western Montana, most of Oregon and northern California mountains down to Calaveras County. Lives near or in water. Toes comparatively long and slender; *distinctive broad, but broken-patterned back stripe, light-colored.*

10.   NORTHWESTERN SALAMANDER, *Ambystoma gracile.* 3 to 4 3/8" long from nose to tail-base. Found in rather narrow coastal strip from western British Columbia south to Sonoma County, California. Likes damp places near water. *Distinctive glandular ridge along upper side of tail* (pits of glands contain whitish poison); color uniform dark brownish above, or spotted with yellowish, pale yellow or bronze specks.

11.   OLYMPIC SALAMANDER, *Rhyacotriton olympicus.* 1½ to 2½"
long from nose to tail-base. Found from Olympic Peninsula in Washington
south through western Washington and Oregon to the northwest corner of
California. Likes fast-flowing, well-shaded, cold streams in coniferous forests, or lives in seepages near such streams. *Small size, short toes, large eyes,
slim body and rather short tail are distinctive.* Color above as shown; yellow-orange on belly. Oregon and California specimens are often more mottled and spotted with dark brown or olive-brown back and head. White flecks
few; belly more greenish-yellow. Very swift swimmer and good runner.

NEWTS

Family Salamandridae—Salamandrids. Skin usually thickened and with
numerous rough warts except in breeding males; *legs comparatively much
stouter than in other salamanders.* Eat insects, worms, etc.

12.   CALIFORNIA NEWT, *Taricha torosa.* 2¾ to 3½" from nose to
tail-base. Found in lower west slopes of Sierra Nevada Mountains in California; also on coast from Sonoma County to San Diego County. Likes
canyon streams where there are oaks and among pines in lower mountain
area. During dry season newts of all species hide in damp cracks, under logs,
etc. At start of rainy season males migrate ahead of females to nearby water where body form changes, thickening around reproductive organs, tail
becomes shaped for fast swimming and skin smoother. Note that *light color
of the upper jaw reaches up to lower eyelid; eyes yellowish to greenish-silver.*

13.   ROUGH-SKINNED NEWT, *Taricha granulosa.* 2¼ to 3½" from
nose to tail-base. Found from British Columbia coast south to Butte and
Santa Cruz counties in California, mainly in coniferous forests, meadows
and grasslands. Black or dark brown above, orange below; *eye yellowish to
pale green. Light color on upper jaw does not extend to lower eyelid.*

14.   RED-BELLIED NEWT, *Taricha rivularis.* 2¾ to 3½". Found along
coast from Humboldt to Sonoma County, California, in redwoods. Uniformly dark brown to black above; *eye dark brown.*

TOADS AND FROGS

Order Salientia—Frogs and Toads. (Lengths are for adults. (See pages 54-57.)
Family Pelobatidae—Spadefoot Toads. Dark spur or spade on hind foot.

15.   PLAINS SPADEFOOT TOAD, *Scaphiopus bombifrons.* 1½ to
2½". Found from southern Alberta, most of Montana east of Rockies and
southwestern South Dakota through Great Plains to southeastern Arizona
and southwest Texas. Hides in holes it digs in grasslands during dry weather,
coming to temporary rain pools to breed. Looks like Western Spadefoot,
but has *high ridge between the eyes.* Male gives hoarse purr or snore.

16.   WESTERN SPADEFOOT, *Scaphiopus hammondi.* 1½ to 2½".
Found in Great Valley and the central and southern coasts of California,
also found from southwest and southeast corners of Colorado, south
and east into western Oklahoma, western Texas, New Mexico and eastern
two-thirds of Arizona, then south into Mexico. Breeds in rain pools of dry
plains and alkali flats; digs holes in dry season. Single, plainly-seen, sharp-
pointed and edged, black spade on hind foot. Variously green, gray or
brown, blotched above, *2 distinctive light stripes on back.* Snoring noise.

21

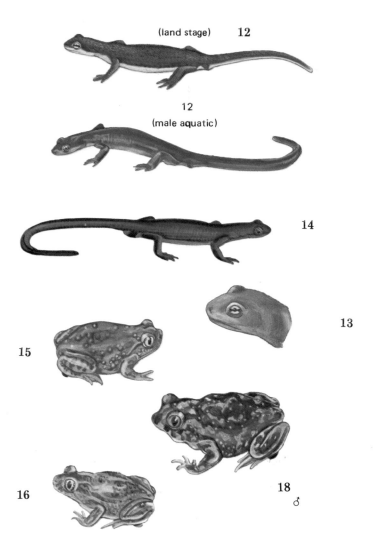

(land stage) 12

12
(male aquatic)

14

13

15

16

18
♂

12. California Newt
13. Rough-skinned Newt
14. Red-bellied Newt
15. Plains Spadefoot Toad
16. Western Spadefoot
18. Couch's Spadefoot

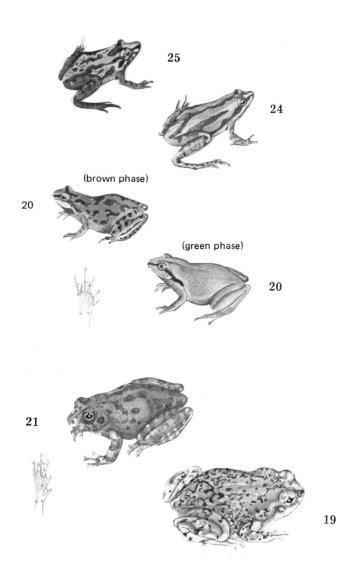

25

24

(brown phase)

20

(green phase)

20

21

19

19. Green Toad
20. Pacific Treefrog
21. Canyon Treefrog
24. Chorus Frog
25. Cricket Frog

17. GREAT BASIN SPADEFOOT TOAD, *Scaphiopus intermontanus.* (Not illus.) 1½ to 2". Has long been considered a subspecies of *S. hammondi,* but is distinguished by a large bump between the eyes. It is found between the Sierra Nevada Mountains and Cascade Ranges on the west and the Rocky Mountains on the east.

18. COUCH'S SPADEFOOT, *Scaphiopus couchi.* 2½ to 3¼". Found from southern Arizona, central New Mexico and western Oklahoma, south through western Texas into northern Mexico. Breeds in temporary pools in semiarid and arid plains and canyons. *Spade on hind foot is curved like a sickle.* Has coarse net-work on back of black to brownish blotches and bars. Male gives moaning or bleating call.

COMMON TOADS, TREEFROGS, AND RELATIVES

Family Bufonidae—Common Toads. (See also pages 56-57.)

19. GREEN TOAD, *Bufo debilis.* 1½ to 2" long. Found from southeastern Arizona, southern and eastern New Mexico, southeastern Colorado, southwestern Kansas and south through western Oklahoma and western two-thirds of Texas into Mexico. Rarely seen except when it rains, living in semiarid and arid mesquite, creosote bush and bunch grass plains. *Large wart-like glands extend from eyes back down shoulders at angle.* Distinctive color pattern as shown. Voice of male sounds like rapidly-repeated one-pitched cricket's trill, or like a cross between a bee's buzz and a whistle.

Family Hylidae—Hylids. Toes with sticky wide tips. Eat insects.

20. PACIFIC TREEFROG, *Hyla regilla.* 5/8 to 2" long. Found from southern British Columbia and Vancouver Island south and west through Washington, Oregon, western Idaho and western Montana to most of Nevada and California, except low deserts. Hides in animal holes, cracks in rocks, etc., near water of ponds, streams, springs, etc. Hind toes webbed with margins distinctly curved in. Colored brownish or greenish, depending on surroundings, with *black mask through eye and Y-shaped blackish or brownish blotch on head.* Mainly active at night. Very powerful, rapidly repeated "krk-ek" call; choruses begin in December or January.

21. CANYON TREEFROG, *Hyla arenicolor.* 1 5/8 to 2". Found from San Luis Obispo County, California south through coastal area to northern Baja California; also from southern Utah and southwestern Colorado through most of Arizona and New Mexico into southwest Texas and Mexico. Prefers rocky, arid or semiarid canyons where there are pools; hides in crevices or perched on rocks; in central Arizona lives in streams among forests. *Eye-stripe usually absent*; distinctive pattern: yellowish and orange on legs; male blackish on throat. Male has quacking call.

22. ARIZONA TREEFROG, *Hyla wrightorum.* (Not illus.) About 2" long. Found through central Arizona and into central west New Mexico; some in southeastern Arizona and north central Mexico, in mountains. Often climbs trees; moves to pools in rainy season. Looks like Pacific Treefrog, but *black eye-stripe extends in trailing spots along side.* Males give 2-12 hoarse metallic clicking clacks.

23. CALIFORNIA TREEFROG, *Hyla californiae.* 1 to 2". (Not illus.) Long considered a subspecies of *H. arenicolor;* gray with darker gray blotches and no eye stripe. Found in southwestern California.

24

24. CHORUS FROG, *Pseudacris triseriata.* 1½ to 2½" long. Found mainly east of line that extends from Alberta south through eastern two-thirds of Montana to southern Idaho, all of Wyoming, most of Colorado, and most of Utah to northern New Mexico and east central Arizona; outside deserts. Likes swamps, marshes, damp meadows and open grasslands, usually on the ground or on plants. Looks like Pacific Treefrog, but has longer eye-stripe, and *usually 5 long dark stripes on grayish, greenish or brownish back.* Voice of male a rapidly repeated vibrating rising chirp.

25. CRICKET FROG, *Acris crepitans.* ¾ to 1¼". From southeast South Dakota, southwest Nebraska, eastern New Mexico and Colorado and most of Texas east into the eastern states and south into Mexico. Damp meadows and swampy places are preferred. Can take enormous jumps for its size. *A light bar on the face reaches from eye to front leg.* Call sounds like 2 stones striking more and more rapidly together.

COMMON FROGS AND TAILED FROG

Family Ranidae—Common Frogs. Very long-legged with webbed hind feet and overall smooth skin. Feed primarily on insects. (See pages 54-55.)

26. BULLFROG, *Rana catesbeiana.* Very large, 6 to 8½". Found in scattered areas throughout the West, where there are large permanent ponds, marshes, etc., but sometimes also in mountain streams. *Eardrums distinctively as large as or larger than eye. Distinct ridge of folded skin behind ear drum.* Male has very deep, hoarse and almost roaring call, like "chug-o-rum!"

27. WOOD FROG, *Rana sylvatica.* 1½ to 3". Found in northern two-thirds of British Columbia, most of Alberta and Saskatchewan and has a local population in the mountains of southeastern Wyoming and north central Colorado. Likes damp forests, but moves to slow streams and ponds to breed. Has distinctive back and side skin folds. Variously colored, but *has very wide dark-brownish eye-mask.* Male gives hoarse, metallic quack.

28. LEOPARD FROG, *Rana pipiens.* 3 to 4". Found over most of West, except California west of Sierras, and western four-fifths of Oregon and Washington, exclusive of middle section along the Columbia River. Adaptable to many habitats wherever there is dampness or water. The *conspicuous oval black spots on back, surrounded by light-colored rings, are distinctive.* Low-pitched, vibrant and throaty moans, grunts and chuckles.

29 SPOTTED FROG, *Rana pretiosa.* 3 to 4". Found in interior British Columbia, southwestern Alberta, eastern two-thirds of Washington, eastern five-sixths of Oregon, most of Idaho, western Montana, western fifth of Wyoming and parts of northern Utah and Nevada, and northeast edge of California, near water. Looks like Red-legged Frog, but *legs are blotched.*

30. FOOTHILL YELLOW-LEGGED FROG, *Rana boylei.* 2 to 3½". Found from Willamette Valley in western Oregon south through foothills, mountains and coniferous forests of California, in slow-flowing creeks, especially those with rocky bottoms, and high mountain lakes. Color on back and head is gray to greenish and reddish-brown, including the ear drums; various amounts of dark spots, bars and markings above contrast with the lighter colors, especially in southern California individuals. *Yellow appears on rear of belly and on hind legs.* Male has gutteral, rasping croak.

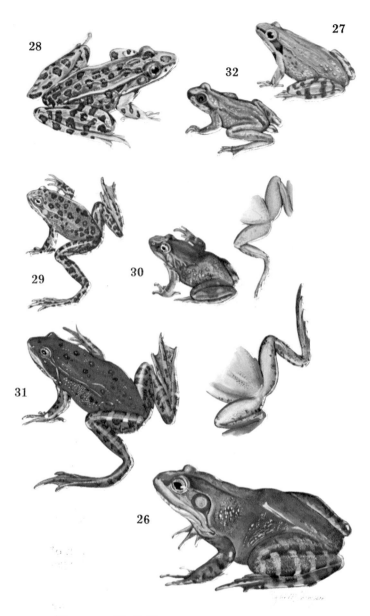

26. Bullfrog
27. Wood Frog
28. Leopard Frog
29. Spotted Frog
30. Foothill Yellow-legged Frog
31. Red-legged Frog
32. Tailed Frog

33. Zebra-tailed Lizard
34. Greater Earless Lizard
35. Lesser Earless Lizard
36. Collared Lizard
37. Leopard Lizard
38. Desert Iguana

31. RED-LEGGED FROG, *Rana aurora*. 4 to 5¼". Found on coast from southwestern British Columbia and Vancouver Island south, including Cascades and Sierras, avoiding Great Valley, to Baja California. Likes quiet permanent bodies of water and damp woods. *Strong skin folds appear on back and sides;* blackish or brownish-black eye mask distinctive; also *whitish streak above mouth;* under surface of *hind legs mainly reddish*, sometimes yellowish. Stutters, grates and growls in 5 to 6 low-pitched gutteral notes.

Family Ascaphidae—Tailed Frogs. "Tail" is really male reproductive organ.

32. TAILED FROG, *Ascaphus truei*. 1¼ to 2" long. Found from southwestern corner of British Columbia along coast south to Mendocino County, California; also in northern Idaho and western sixth of Montana. Likes permanent, swift-flowing streams in coniferous forests. *Distinctive vertical pupil in eye is oval in shape; broad fifth toe.*

REPTILES

Class Reptilia—Reptiles. (See pages 58-73.) (Sizes given are of adults.)
Order Squamata—Lizards and Snakes. (See pages 58-73.)
Suborder Sauria—Lizards. (See pages 58-65.)

IGUANID LIZARDS

Family Iguanidae—Iguanid Lizards. Scales tough and hard to touch.

33. ZEBRA-TAILED LIZARD, *Callisaurus draconoides*. 2½ to 3½" from nose to tail-base. Found from central west Nevada south and east to southeastern California, the southwestern tip of Utah, west, central and south Arizona. Likes sandy, gravelly and lightly rocky deserts. *Upper lip scales separated by slanting lines; distinctive black rings on tail.*

34. GREATER EARLESS LIZARD, *Holbrookia texana*. 2¼ to 3" from nose to tail-base. Found from central Arizona south and east to northern Mexico, south half of New Mexico and central and southwestern Texas. Likes rocky hillsides, canyons and arid or semiarid flats with scattered brush. Looks like Zebra-tailed Lizard, but has *no apparent ear openings.*

35. LESSER EARLESS LIZARD, *Holbrookia maculata*. 2 to 2½" from nose to tail-base. Found from southern South Dakota, the west four-fifths of Nebraska and the southeast corner of Wyoming south and west to the western two-thirds of Kansas, Texas, eastern and southwestern Colorado, southwestern Utah, most of New Mexico, eastern and Grand Canyon area of Arizona, and western and central Mexico. Likes gravelly and sparsely vegetated sandy areas of deserts and plains, but also rocky areas and canyons of low mountains. Looks like Side-blotched Lizard (see page 31), but has *no ear opening and upper lip scales are overlapping.* Eats insects.

36. COLLARED LIZARD, *Crotaphytus collaris*. 3½ to 4½" from nose to tail-base. Found from southeastern Oregon and southern Idaho south and east through northeastern and southeastern California, then east to eastern two-thirds of Texas, Oklahoma, central Kansas and central and northwestern Mexico. Likes semiarid and arid rocky hills or mountains; rare in plains except where there are rocky canyons, gullies and rock piles; occasionally found in sandy places. Variously colored, but usually has *2 distinctive black collar bands.* Very aggressive, fast hunter of small lizards.

37.　LEOPARD LIZARD, *Crotaphytus wislizenii*. 3½ to 4½" from base of tail to nose. Found from central north Oregon and southern Idaho south through eastern California, the San Joaquin Valley and southeast California, then east to southwest Texas and western Colorado and north central Mexico in semiarid and arid, sparsely-vegetated and usually sandy or gravelly plains; rarer in sand dunes or rocky areas. *Has distinctive brownish-black spots and white cross-bars.* Fast hunter of lizards.

38.　DESERT IGUANA, *Dipsosaurus dorsalis*. 4 to 5½". Found from southern Nevada and southeastern California south into eastern Baja California and west into western Arizona and Sonora. *Row of enlarged keeled scales down back.* Also has unusual color design, as shown, and distinctively barred tail. Feeds mainly in daylight on plants and their flowers.

39.　CLARK'S SPINY LIZARD, *Sceloporus clarki*. 3 to 5" from nose to base of tail. Found from central Arizona and southwest New Mexico south into central and western Mexico. Likes to climb in trees and on rocks in semiarid and arid areas. Looks like Desert Spiny Lizard, but has *3 enlarged scales just in front of ear, usually with rounded ends,* and has quite plainly seen *black to dark brown slanting marks on the wrists and forearms.* General color may vary from green to bluish-green to gray. Most spiny lizards eat insects, etc.; some catch smaller lizards.

40.　DESERT SPINY LIZARD, *Sceloporus magister*. 3½ to 5½" from nose to tail-base. Found from west central Nevada and the San Joaquin Valley, California south and east through southeast California, southern Utah, the southwest corner of Colorado, Arizona and northwest and southern New Mexico to southwest Texas and north central and northwest Mexico. Likes rocky and sparsely vegetated deserts and semiarid regions, but not completely barren. Often climbs trees and steep rocks. *5 to 7 enlarged scales, usually pointed, in front of ears. The black mark on the shoulder has a light yellowish or whitish edging behind it;* general color above is pale yellow to brownish-yellow.

41.　CREVICE SPINY LIZARD, *Sceloporus poinsetti*. 3¾ to 5" from nose to tail-base. Found from southern New Mexico and southwest and south central Texas south into central northeast Mexico. Likes to hide in crevices of rock outcrops in semiarid and desert regions, sometimes in mountains. *The distinctive broad, black collar on neck is edged with lighter color in front and behind.* Color gray-olive to yellow; markedly banded tail.

42.　YARROW'S SPINY LIZARD, *Sceloporus jarrovi*. 2½ to 3½". Found in mountains of southeast Arizona, southwest New Mexico and north central Mexico. Likes oak and coniferous forests where there are rock piles and cliffs. Has very *striking pattern of whitish or pink black-edged scales;* has dark collar like Crevice Spiny Lizard, but no light area in front. Climbs trees.

43.　GRANITE SPINY LIZARD, *Sceloporus orcutti*. 3 to 4" from nose to base of tail. Found from San Gorgonio Pass in southern California south through the lower interior mountains and their foothills to and throughout Baja California. *Best told by its habitat in the piles of granite rocks on chaparral-covered hillsides.* Also is usually quite dark in color and the scales on the back are weakly tipped and keeled (sometimes no keels). Males have strong blue coloring underneath.

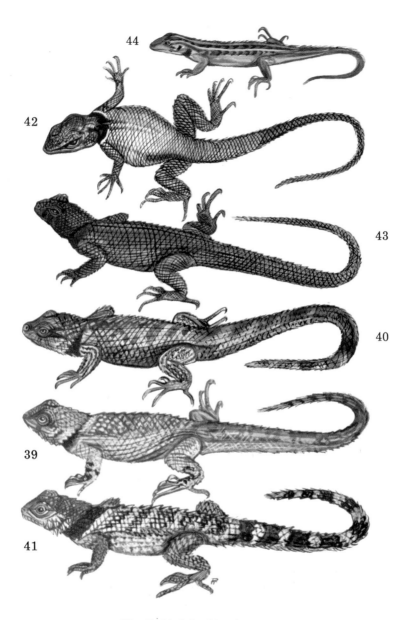

39. Clark's Spiny Lizard
40. Desert Spiny Lizard
41. Crevice Spiny Lizard
42. Yarrow's Spiny Lizard
43. Granite Spiny Lizard
44. Bunch Grass Lizard

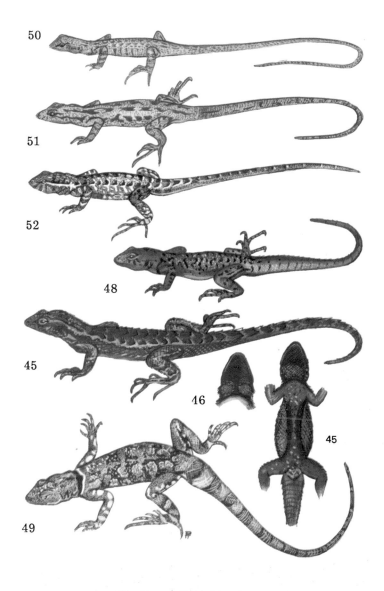

45. Western Fence Lizard
46. Eastern Fence Lizard
48. Sagebrush Lizard
49. Banded Rock Lizard
50. Long-tailed Brush Lizard
51. Tree Lizard
52. Side-blotched Lizard

31

44.   BUNCH GRASS LIZARD, *Sceloporus scalaris*. 1 7/8 to 2½" from nose to tail-base. Found in mountains of southeast Arizona and north central Mexico. Likes bunch grass clearings in high mountain coniferous forests, often hiding under rocks or logs or in bunches of grass. It is different from other western Sceloporus lizards because of the *side scales being parallel with those on back instead of coming up to them at an angle.* The four whitish stripes on the light-brown back are distinctive; the male has heavier blue on the belly than female and differs as shown.

45.   WESTERN FENCE LIZARD, *Sceloporus occidentalis*. 2¼ to 3½" from nose to base of tail. Found from central and southern Washington, except coast, east to southwest Idaho and south through most of Oregon, except northwest coast and high mountains, to Nevada, west edge of Utah, most of California except the southeast deserts, and on to northern Baja California. Likes wooded and rocky areas, old buildings, etc. *Large scales above eyes are separated from large head plates by half-circle of small scales;* many pointed and keeled scales reach down thigh. Male usually has 2 dark blue patches on belly and one on throat; blue on female much less. Lizards on this page eat mainly insects, spiders, etc.

46.   EASTERN FENCE LIZARD, *Sceloporus undulatus*. 2¼ to 3½" from nose to tail-base. Found south and east of southern and eastern Utah, southeast and southwest Wyoming, southwest South Dakota, western ¾ of Nebraska and all of Kansas. Likes many habitats, but especially rocks, brush, deciduous woods and lower coniferous forests. Very similar to Western Fence Lizard, so best told by locality, but males usually have 2 wedge-like blue throat patches instead of one.

47.   STRIPED PLATEAU LIZARD, *Sceloporus virgatus*. (Not illus.) Long considered a subspecies of *S. undulatus*, lives in mountains of southwestern New Mexico and southeastern Arizona; lacks blue blotches on belly.

48.   SAGEBRUSH LIZARD, *Sceloporus graciosus*. 2 to 2½" from nose to tail-base. Found inland in mountains and foothills of California (mountains only in south), also in eastern two-thirds of Oregon and central eastern Washington, then south and east in mountain and high plateau areas to south central Montana, western Wyoming and Colorado and northern Arizona and New Mexico. An isolated population in southeast New Mexico. Likes sagebrush and pinyon-juniper-covered flats and hillsides and open coniferous forests, hiding in rocks, brush, litter, stumps, etc. *Most scales on thigh smooth, not keeled; usually rust-colored at base of legs.*

49.   BANDED ROCK LIZARD, *Petrosaurus   mearnsi*. 3 to 4" from nose to base of tail. Found in rocky areas, particularly in desert canyons from Palm Springs area in Riverside County, California, south along western edge of Sonoran Desert into Baja California. Looks something like Collared Lizard (page 27), but has *only one black collar* (bordered behind by white); has *black bands on tail.*

50.   LONG-TAILED BRUSH LIZARD, *Urosaurus graciosus*. 2 to 2¼" long from nose to base of tail. Found from extreme south Nevada through southeastern California and western Arizona into northwest Mexico. Likes desert scrub and loose sand, and can change color to suit environment. Tail often over twice as long as the head and body together; *a broad band of larger, keeled and overlapping scales extends down middle of back.*

32

51.   TREE LIZARD, *Urosaurus ornatus.* 1¾ to 2¼" from nose to tail-base.   Found from extreme southeast California and southern Nevada east through southern and eastern Utah, west fifth of Colorado, Arizona, western two-thirds of New Mexico and southwest and south central Texas into Mexico.   Climbs rocks, bushes and trees.   *Has strip of large scales on back divided by line of small scales.*   Blue belly patches on male.

52.   SIDE-BLOTCHED LIZARD, · *Uta stansburiana.*   1¾ to 2½" long from nose to tail-base.   Found from east south central Washington south through eastern Oregon, southern Idaho and southwest Wyoming, Utah, Nevada, eastern and southwestern California into Arizona, New Mexico, west Texas and Mexico.   Likes sand, gravel and rocks in desert and semi-desert areas.   *Black spot behind front leg on side.*

SKINKS AND ALLIGATOR LIZARDS

Family Scincidae—Skinks.   Smooth scales shaped like tiny meat choppers. Very secretive hiders under boards, stones, etc.   Eat insects, worms, snails, etc.

53.   GILBERT'S SKINK, *Eumeces gilberti.*   2½ to 4½" from nose to tail-base.   Found from Yuba County in the Sacramento Valley south to Sacramento area and then by way of the foothills surrounding San Joaquin Valley to the Tehachapi Mountains and the mountains of southern California; also in Inyo County, California, in Clark and Nye Counties, Nevada, and Yavapai County, Arizona.   Likes dry forests and grasslands.   *Upper lip scales usually 8;* otherwise very similar to Western Skink, but adults lose side stripes, and young of Gilbert's Skinks have reddish tails where the two are found together; elsewhere both have blue tails.

54.   WESTERN SKINK, *Eumeces skiltonianus.*   2¼ to 3¼" from nose to tail-base.   Likes damper areas rarely occupied by similar Gilbert's Skink, from southern British Columbia south through the eastern two-thirds of Washington, Idaho, western fifth of Montana, all of Oregon except northwest corner, western Utah, northern two-thirds of Nevada plus Charleston Mountains in south, then northern and coastal California down to Baja California.   *Generally has 7 upper lip scales;* the 2 long light-colored stripes on sides are kept in adults; blue tail found in young.

55.   GREAT PLAINS SKINK, *Eumeces obsoletus.*   3½ to 5" long. Found from central and southeastern Arizona through most of New Mexico, eastern Colorado, southern Nebraska, Kansas, Oklahoma and western two-thirds of Texas south into Mexico.   Likes woodlands and grasslands.   *Distinctive slanting upwards of scales on sides of body.*   Young have orange and white spots on head.

56.   MANY-LINED SKINK, *Eumeces multivirgatus.*   2 to 3" from nose to tail-base.   Found from southwest South Dakota and southeast Wyoming, south through western Nebraska, northwest Kansas and eastern Colorado to northern and central Arizona and New Mexico and a corner of southwest Texas.   Likes short grass prairies.   *Told from other skinks by numerous dark and light stripes, one running exactly along one row of scales and 3 scale rows away from mid-line of back.*

57.   MOUNTAIN SKINK, *Eumeces callicephalus.*   (Not illus.)   Often with light Y marks on head, is found in mountains of s.e. Arizona.

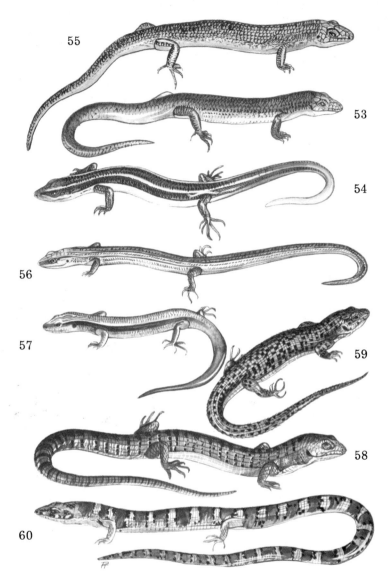

55

53

54

56

57

59

58

60

53. Gilbert's Skink
54. Western Skink
55. Great Plains Skink
56. Many-lined Skink
57. Mountain Skink
58. Southern Alligator Lizard
59. Northern Alligator Lizard
60. Arizona Alligator Lizard

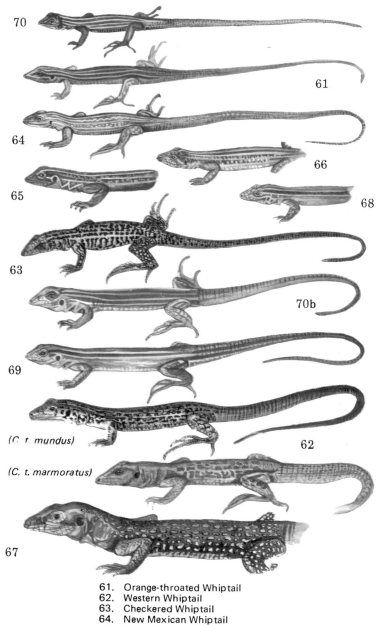

(C. t. mundus)

(C. t. marmoratus)

61. Orange-throated Whiptail
62. Western Whiptail
63. Checkered Whiptail
64. New Mexican Whiptail
65. Texas Spotted Whiptail
66. Chihuahua Whiptail
67. Giant Spotted Whiptail
68. Plateau Whiptail
69. Six-lined Racerunner
70. Little Striped Whiptail
70b. Desert-grassland Whiptail

Family Anguidae—Alligator Lizards. Rather short legs, *fold of skin prominent on side;* feed mainly on insects and worms; hiss defiantly at enemies.

58. SOUTHERN ALLIGATOR LIZARD, *Gerrhonotus multicarinatus.* 4 to 6½" from nose to tail-base. Found from central Columbia River Valley in Washington and Oregon south down Willamette Valley to coast of northern California and all of California west of high mountains, except San Joaquin Valley, on south to Baja California. Likes woods, grasslands and brush. *Distinctive longitudinal dark lines through centers of belly scales.*

59. NORTHERN ALLIGATOR LIZARD, *Gerrhonotus coeruleus.* 3½ to 5½" from nose to tail-base. Found from southern British Columbia, northern Idaho and western quarter of Montana south through western Washington and Oregon to mountain and hill country in northern California. Usually found under objects in moist coniferous woods. *Distinctive longitudinal dark lines run along edges of belly scales.*

60. ARIZONA ALLIGATOR LIZARD, *Gerrhonotus kingi.* 3 to 5" from nose to tail-base. Central and southeast Arizona, southwest New Mexico, north central Mexico, in oaks, grass, brush. *Irregular dark marks on belly.*

WHIPTAIL AND RACERUNNER LIZARDS

Family Teidae—Teid Lizards. Belly scales quadrangular, not overlapping and commonly in 8 longitudinal rows. Eat mainly insects; fast runners.

61. ORANGE-THROATED WHIPTAIL, *Cnemidophorus hyperythrus.* 2 to 2½" from nose to tail-base. Found from western Riverside County, California south to coast in San Diego County and in Baja California and east to edge of desert. Likes rocky and brushy areas of semiarid and arid regions in loose sandy soil. Distinctive single rather than divided plate in middle of head between eyes. Other Whiptail Lizards have this plate divided.

62. WESTERN WHIPTAIL, *Cnemidophorus tigris.* 2¾ to 4" from nose to tail-base. Found over most of California except northwest coast and high Sierras; also in southeast Oregon, southwest Idaho, Nevada, most of Utah, Arizona, southwest Colorado, northwest and south New Mexico, then in southwest Texas and northern Mexico. Likes many habitats, but particularly dry sandy and rocky areas, brushy arroyos and washes. Has 4 longitudinal stripes of lighter color; numerous black spots on light blue to gray, white or yellow undersides.

63. CHECKERED WHIPTAIL, *Cnemidophorus tesselatus.* 3 to 4" from nose to tail-base. Found from southeastern Colorado south to western tip of Oklahoma, western and south central New Mexico, western Texas and north central Mexico. Likes canyons with scattered brush and grassy hills with few trees. *Looks like Western Whiptail, but dark and white barring on the back is heavier and more contrasty, while belly has fewer spots.*

64. NEW MEXICAN WHIPTAIL, *Cnemidophorus neomexicanus.* 2¼ to 3" from nose to tail-base. Found in small region of central and south west New Mexico. Likes edges of desert washes. *Two lines of small scales curve far forward in middle of head;* pattern of 7 stripes on back appears light-dotted; tail blue.

65. TEXAS SPOTTED WHIPTAIL, *Cnemidophorus gularis.* 2½ to 3½" from nose to tail-base. Found over most of Texas except upper panhandle and eastern fifth of state, then south into northeastern Mexico.

Prefers grassy prairies, particularly in or near washes and river bottom land, also in brushy areas and with cacti, mesquite and acacia. *Has 7-8 back stripes, with fainter, broader back stripe; dark areas with yellowish-brown spots.* Tail of young reddish, while adult's tail fades from red to brown. In western Texas may be confused with Chihuahua Whiptail, which is closely related, but the latter is found in higher more desert-like areas.

66.   CHIHUAHUA WHIPTAIL, *Cnemidophorus exsanguis.* 3 to 3¾" from nose to tail-base. Found from western Texas to central Arizona and north central New Mexico, also south into bordering areas of Mexico. Prefers higher deserts and grassland areas, reaching also upward into pine-oak woods and lower mountain yellow pine forests. Similar to above lizard, but generally has *6 light stripes on back, but dark areas with yellowish-brown spots. Very large scales are found on back side of forearm.* Central stripe often indistinct, narrow or turning into a line of spots or even no longer present.

67.   GIANT SPOTTED WHIPTAIL, *Cnemidophorus burti.* 3½ to 5½" from nose to tail-base. Found in mountain areas of southern Arizona and extreme southwestern corner of New Mexico south into Mexican mountains. Prefers desert-like mountain canyons, arroyos and mesas, usually in thick scrub; sometimes in grass near streams and in oak woods. *Very similar to 66, but generally larger and with fainter or absent stripes, particularly in the large adults; stripes when present 6-7; back usually light-spotted in dark areas; upper parts often reddish in part or whole.*

68.   PLATEAU WHIPTAIL, *Cnemidophorus velox.* 2½ to 3½" from nose to tail-base. Found in high plateau and mountainous areas from central Arizona and northwest New Mexico north into southern Utah and southeastern Colorado. Prefers oak and pinyon-juniper woods, lower altitudes of yellow pine forests and sometimes streamside woods of lower areas. *Similar to 66, but lacks large scales on back of forearm, and dark areas between the 6-7 light back stripes have no light spots; tail distinctively light bluish.*

69.   SIX-LINED RACERUNNER, *Cnemidophorus sexlineatus.* 2½ to 3¼" from nose to tail-base. Found from southeast Wyoming, southern South Dakota, eastern Colorado, the northeast corner of New Mexico, and northern and eastern Texas, into the east. Likes many habitats, but prefers drier more open areas with scattered brush and trees. *The Texas Spotted Whiptail is the only related species in part of same area, but sexlineatus has no white spots on dark stripes and has much smaller scales on back of forearm.*

70.   LITTLE STRIPED WHIPTAIL, *Cnemidophorus inornatus.* 2 to 2¾" from nose to tail-base. Found from central Rio Grande Valley and northwest corner of New Mexico and southeast corner of Arizona south into north central Mexico and east into southwest Texas. Likes plains with low-growing bushes, and juniper tree grasslands of lower mountains. *Tail, head, legs and lower surfaces with light blue suffusion or tinge.*

70b. DESERT-GRASSLAND WHIPTAIL, *Cnemidophorus uniparens.* Size and appearance as above, except tail greenish to bluish-olive. Desert grass and oak woods in southern Arizona and New Mexico.

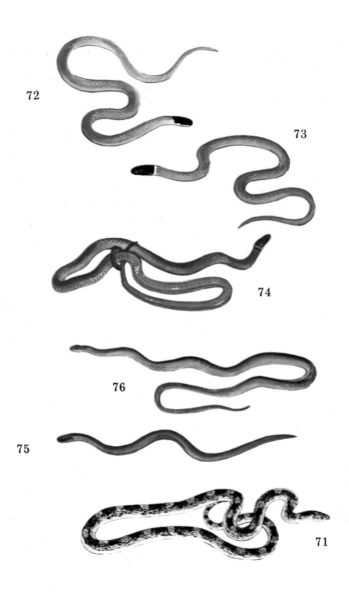

72

73

74

76

75

71

71. Long-nosed Snake
72. Plains Black-headed Snake
73. Western Black-headed Snake
74. Ringneck Snake
75. Sharp-tailed Snake
76. Smooth Green Snake

38

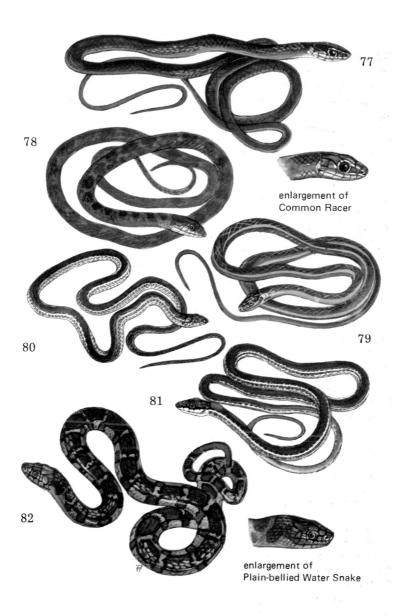

enlargement of
Common Racer

enlargement of
Plain-bellied Water Snake

77. Common Racer
78. Coachwhip
79. Striped Racer
80. Striped Whipsnake
81. Sonora Whipsnake
82. Plain-bellied Water Snake

COMMON SNAKES

Suborder Serpentes—Snakes. (See pages 64-73.) Lengths are of adults.
Family Colubridae—Colubrid or Common Snakes. (See pages 70-73.)

71. LONG-NOSED SNAKE, *Rhinocheilus lecontei.* 2 to 3¼'. Widespread in arid and semiarid plains and foothill regions of the west from southeast Kansas, east central Texas, and northeast Mexico to southeast Idaho, northwest Nevada and California. Belly and tail scales usually all single (see page 12). *Distinctive black saddles on back separated by light color.* Feeds mainly on lizards.

72. PLAINS BLACK-HEADED SNAKE, *Tantilla nigriceps.* 9 to 14" long. Found from southeastern Arizona, northeast Mexico, western two-thirds of Texas, south and eastern New Mexico, and eastern Colorado, east to Kansas and southwest Nebraska. Hides under stones and in burrows mainly in short grass plains. *Black on top of head extends farther back into small scales of back than any other black-headed snake.* Feeds on spiders, worms, slugs, insects, etc. as do similar species.

73. WESTERN BLACK-HEADED SNAKE, *Tantilla planiceps.* 8 to 15" long. Found in scattered drier areas of California from Livermore Valley south to northwestern Baja California; some in Inyo and San Luis Obispo Counties; southern Nevada Mountains, southern Utah, southern Arizona and New Mexico, far west Texas pan-handle and parts of north central Mexico. Usually found hiding under rocks or debris, in animal burrows, in grassy, brushy woodland and desert areas; may be especially common near streams and damp washes. Comes out from hiding to hunt on warm nights. Has *distinctive blackish cap*, which varies in shape among its four subspecies as shown in the color plate; there is *usually a whitish collar behind the black cap*, body generally brownish above to grayish-olive, sometimes with faint back stripe.

74. RINGNECK SNAKE, *Diadophis punctatus.* 11 to 31" in length. Very widespread in scattered areas of west, including southern Washington, western Oregon, northwest and southern Idaho, coastal and foothill California, east edge of Nevada, central Utah, low mountain and plateau areas of Arizona and New Mexico, Texas except far eastern part, southeastern Colorado, and into the midwest. Likes moist woodlands, lower coniferous forests and brushlands, hiding beneath rocks, boards, in burrows, etc., but coming out on warm nights to hunt worms, frogs, lizards, salamanders, smaller snakes, and insects. *Distinctive bright yellow-orange or coral red color of the belly reaches up to the lower rows of upper body scales; the bright orange or yellow neck ring* may be absent in some areas, particularly southern New Mexico.

75. SHARP-TAILED SNAKE, *Contia tenuis.* 10 to 16". Found in scattered areas from southeastern Vancouver Island, south shore of Puget Sound in Washington, Jackson and Benton Counties in Oregon, and south in California among lower mountains and foothills to Monterey and Fresno Counties. Found under surface objects in damp woods and brush. Feeds on worms, slugs and salamanders. *Distinctive spine on tail.*

76. SMOOTH GREEN SNAKE, *Opheodrys vernalis.* 12 to 24". Found in scattered areas of south and central New Mexico, western two-thirds of Colorado, northeast Utah, southern and eastern Wyoming, southwest South Dakota, and to the east. Likes moist grasslands, meadows, marshes, etc. *Distinctive uniform green above, pale colors below.* Very secretive.

77. COMMON RACER, *Coluber constrictor.* 2½ to 4½'. Found in south central British Columbia and over most of the western U.S. except the most humid northwest coast, the drier deserts, the higher Rocky Mountains, and a section of eastern New Mexico and southwest Texas. Likes open brushland, grassland, and open forests. Very fast snake and good climber, hunting amphibians, small reptiles and mammals. *Of the 2 scales in front of the eye, the lower one is small and wedged between 2 of the upper lip scales.*

78. COACHWHIP, *Masticophis flagellum.* 3 to 6' long. Found all across the southern half of the western U.S. and Mexico, avoiding the humid coast belt in California and the higher mountains in a line from Sacramento and Reno west through southern Utah, southwest and southeast Colorado, southwest Nebraska and Kansas into the eastern states. Likes brushy deserts, short-grass prairies, dry grasslands, chaparral, etc. *Unlike other whipsnakes, it has no stripes, but dark cross-bands instead, especially in neck area.* Feeds on rodents, birds, eggs, snakes, large insects, etc.

79. STRIPED RACER, *Masticophis lateralis.* 2½ to 5¼'. Found in coastal and foothill California, outside of the Great Valley, the humid northwest coast and the deserts. Likes brush best, oaks second. A good climber, hunting birds, snakes, lizards, frogs, rodents and insects. *Has distinctive yellow or cream-colored single stripe on each side.*

80. STRIPED WHIPSNAKE, *Masticophis taeniatus.* 3 to 5½' long. Found from south central Washington south through eastern Oregon, southern Idaho, eastern edge of California along Nevada border, Nevada, Utah, southeastern Wyoming, eastern quarter of Colorado, northern and central eastern Arizona, western and southern New Mexico, southern and southwestern Texas and northeastern Mexico. Likes sagebrush desert, rocky canyons, yellow pine and oak forests. *Differs from other whipsnakes by having usually 15 rows of scales across the middle of the body; also the white stripe on side usually has a dark often broken line down its middle.* Food as above.

81. SONORA WHIPSNAKE, *Masticophis bilineatus.* 3 to 4½'. Found in middle, south and southeast Arizona, southwest New Mexico and Sonora, Mexico. Likes rocky canyons, chaparral, oak woods, and sahuaro-palo verde-ocotillo high deserts. *Body appears longitudinally streaked light and dark with flecked appearance.* Eats birds and lizards.

82. PLAIN-BELLIED WATER SNAKE, *Natrix erythrogaster.* (See pages 68-69.) 2½ to 5'. Found from the southeast corner of New Mexico south and east through most of Texas, northeast Mexico, Oklahoma, south and northeast Kansas into the eastern states. Like ponds, streams, lakes, etc. Unlike the similar garter snakes, the *anal plate has 2 divisions* (see page 12). Scales keeled. Usually uniformly black, gray or reddish-brown above, but sometimes with row of square blotches down back. Feeds on water creatures.

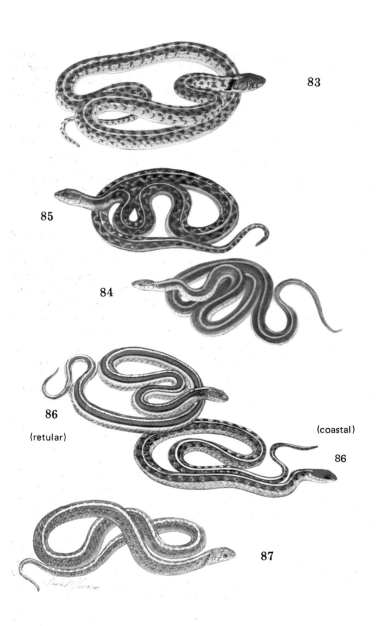

83

85

84

86

(retular)

(coastal)

86

87

83. Checkered Garter Snake
84. Western Aquatic Garter Snake
85. Western Terrestrial Garter Snake
86. Common Garter Snake
87. Northwestern Garter Snake

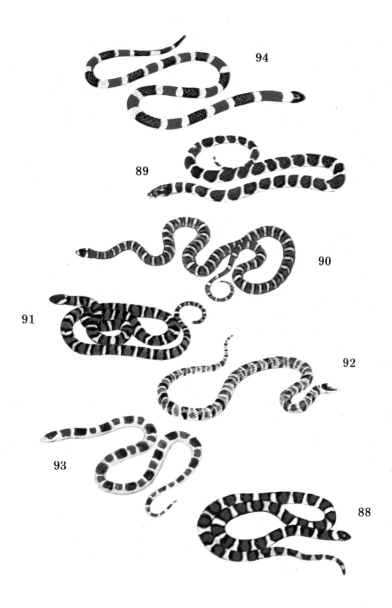

88. Milk Snake
89. Common Kingsnake
90. Sonora Mountain Kingsnake
91. California Mountain Kingsnake
92. Western Shovel-nosed Snake
93. Sonora Shovel-nosed Snake
94. Arizona Coral Snake

83.　CHECKERED GARTER SNAKE, *Thamnophis marcianus.* 1½ to 2¼'. All garter snakes have keeled scales, but usually one anal plate. Found from southeast California,east and south through southern Arizona, southern and northeast New Mexico, southeast Colorado, southwest Kansas, western Oklahoma and western three-quarters of Texas, and much of northern Mexico. Likes lowland waterways. *Two checker-like rows of black blotches on back; light-colored crescents on neck just back of head.* Eats amphibians, lizards, etc.

84.　WESTERN AQUATIC GARTER SNAKE, *Thamnophis couchi.* 1½ to 5'. Usually 8 upper lip scales. Found from southwestern Oregon south through most of California except the southeast and northeast desert areas. A more narrow head than above snake and with long narrow scales between the nostrils on the forehead; body less striped and more spotted. Especially eat fish and frogs. Usually found in or near water.

85.　WESTERN TERRESTRIAL GARTER SNAKE, *Thamnophis elegans.* 1½ to 3½'. *Usually 8 upper lip scales.* They have broad heads with scales as broad as they are long between the nostrils. The terrestrial snakes are found in the mountain and foothill sections of California, most of Oregon and Washington except part of the Cascades in Oregon and the mid coastal strip, then north into southern British Columbia and east to southwest Alberta, western and southern Montana, eastern South Dakota and Nebraska, western three-quarters of Colorado and northern four-fifths of New Mexico. They like damp meadows and streamside woods. They usually have a broad light stripe down their back except for the form found in north central and northeast California.

86.　COMMON GARTER SNAKE, *Thamnophis sirtalis.* 2 to 4'. Found over much of the western U.S. and Canada with the exception of Arizona, most of Utah, southeastern California and other dry areas. Likes meadows, marshes, ponds, streams, and streamside brush. Very aggressive, often biting. *Most often has 7 upper lip scales. Usually red-marked or even red-striped on sides.* May be black, bluish, gray or brown on back with broad pale stripe down middle.

87.　NORTHWESTERN GARTER SNAKE, *Thamnophis ordinoides.* 15 to 20". Found from southwest British Columbia and Vancouver Island south through western third of Washington and Oregon to northwest tip of California. Likes damp meadows and other openings in dense humid forests. Much less pugnacious than Western Terrestrial Garter Snake, smaller in size, has *7 upper lip scales* instead of 8, and always has a middle back stripe of red, orange, yellow or blue; often with brilliant red spots and black marks.

KINGSNAKES, SHOVEL-NOSED SNAKES, CORAL, CORN
AND GLOSSY SNAKES

88.　MILK SNAKE, *Lampropeltis triangulum.* 1½ to 4¼'. Found from central Utah and northeast Arizona, eastern Wyoming, southern Montana, and parts of New Mexico into the east. Likes many habitats, particularly woods and canyons; active at night. *Red bands on back appear more X-shaped than in the Mountain Kingsnakes.*

89. COMMON KINGSNAKE, *Lampropeltis getulus.* 2½ to 3¼'. Found from central southwest Oregon, central west Nevada, southeast Utah, northwest and central Arizona, central New Mexico, central Texas, most of Oklahoma and Kansas, and eastern Nebraska south into Mexico and east into the eastern states. Lives in many habitats from forests to deserts. *Dark above with light-colored cross-bands or light stripe down middle of back* (southwest California), and also an all-black form. The smooth shiny scales, single anal plate (page 12), and the dark-marked pale belly are characteristic of all Kingsnakes. Most Kingsnakes eat small rodents, snakes, lizards, birds.

90. SONORA MOUNTAIN KINGSNAKE, *Lampropeltis pyromelana.* 1½ to 2¼'. Found in mountains down center of Utah, then skips the Grand Canyon and is found from south rim down through central and eastern Arizona to southeast New Mexico and central north Mexico in mountains. Likes pinyon-juniper, fir and pine forests and chaparral. Differs from similar California Mountain Kingsnake by having *light colored nose and black bands narrowing on sides.*

91. CALIFORNIA MOUNTAIN KINGSNAKE, *Lampropeltis zonata.* 1½ to 2½'. Found from Mt. Adams region of Washington south in mountains to mountains of California and Baja California. Likes yellow pine forests, but also found in chaparral and live oaks. *Black nose and black banding, split by red and surrounded by white rings, is very similar to Milk Snake,* but living range of two snakes entirely different. The form in Yosemite region has no red in color, and looks like Common Kingsnake, but has no white on the nose. (Yellow-bellied Kingsnake, *L. calligaster* of Kansas, has distinctive dark or brown blotches on back edged with black.)

92. WESTERN SHOVEL-NOSED SNAKE, *Chionactis occipitalis.* 10 to 16". Found from southwest Nevada south into southeast California, southwest Arizona and northwest Mexico in desert areas. Likes sandy and barren desert, also brushy desert, and less often lives in rocky and grassy areas, hunting mainly insects and related animals; the snake often burrows in sand. *Back patterned with 21 or more black or brown cross-bands on yellow to white ground color;* smooth scales; lower jaw looks as though it runs up into upper jaw.

93. SONORA SHOVEL-NOSED SNAKE, *Chionactis palarostris.* 10 to 16". Found in small area in south central Arizona and south into Sonora, Mexico. Like above snake, but *black cross-bands are 10 to 20.* (Compare the Shovel-nosed Snakes on page 43 with the Banded Sand Snake shown on page 68.)

Family Elapidae—Elpids. Poisonous, rigid, hollow fangs in front of mouth.

94. ARIZONA CORAL SNAKE, *Micruroides euryxanthus.* 12 to 20". Found in central and southeast Arizona, southwest New Mexico and northwest Mexico, in semiarid and desert country up to 5,000 feet altitude. *Bright and broad red bands around body are bordered on each side by smaller yellow or whitish bands,* thus very different from Mountain Kingsnakes and Milk Snakes (as shown). The Shovel-nosed Snakes and the Banded Sand Snakes are also similar, but bands on these snakes are only saddles, not complete red rings, and they also have white snouts. Feeds mainly on snakes and lizards.

45

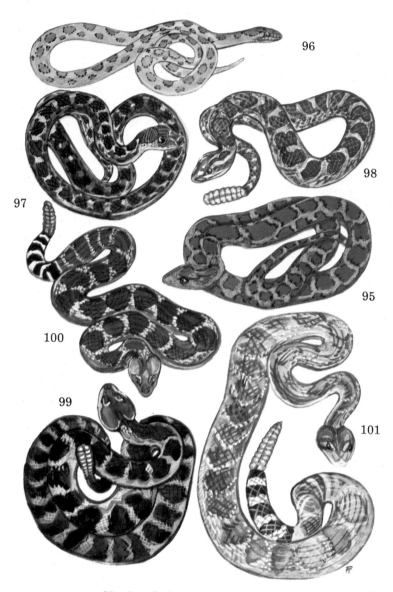

96

98

97

95

100

99

101

95. Corn Snake
96. Glossy Snake
97. Gopher Snake
98. Massasauga
99. Western Rattlesnake
100. Red Diamond Rattlesnake
101. Western Diamondback Rattlesnake

102. Yellow Mud Turtle
103. Western Box Turtle
104. Painted Turtle
105. Western Pond Turtle
106. Pond Slider
107. Spiny Softshell Turtle

47

95. CORN SNAKE, *Elaphe guttata.* 2½ to 6'. Found in small area on middle Utah-Colorado border; also in southeast Colorado, most of Kansas, Oklahoma, Texas, west two-thirds of New Mexico, and northeast Mexico. Anal plate divided; back scales weakly keeled; the 42 to 45 brown, generally oval blotches edged with black or dark brown are distinctive. Feeds mainly on small mammals.

96. GLOSSY SNAKE, *Arizona elegans.* 2½ to 4¾'. Found in desert areas and southern coastal foothills of south half of California, southern Nevada, west and central Arizona, central, southern and eastern New Mexico, Kansas, Oklahoma and most of Texas. Likes sandy areas, more rarely rocky places and brush or fields. *Lower jaw seems pressed into upper jaw; smooth scales; 55-60 back blotches.* Feeds on lizards mainly, also small mammals.

GOPHER SNAKES, RATTLESNAKES

97. GOPHER SNAKE, *Pituophis melanoleucus.* 2½ to 8' long. Found in southwest Canada and over most of western U.S. except northwest corner of Oregon, western third of Washington, and high mountain areas in California, Wyoming and Colorado. Adaptable to many habitats, feeds mainly in daytime on small mammals. Vibrating of tail in leaves plus color pattern of dark brown blotches on lighter body make many people think it is a rattlesnake on first sight, but neck and head are near same width. *Scales on back keeled; 4 large scales just behind scales that touch nose openings.*

Family Crotalidae—Pit Vipers (see description on pages 70-73). Poisonous.

98. MASSASAUGA, *Sistrurus catenatus.* 2 to 3¼'. Found from southeast Arizona, southern and eastern New Mexico through most of western and central Texas, Oklahoma, southeast Colorado, Kansas and southeast Nebraska into the middle western states. Likes swamps and other damp localities. Different from other rattlesnakes because of the *9 large plates on head.* Poisonous.

99. WESTERN RATTLESNAKE, *Crotalus viridis.* 1½ to 5'. Found in south central British Columbia, southern Alberta and southwest Saskatchewan, and over most of western U.S. except the humid northwest coast, the hot, low deserts of California, Arizona and southern Nevada, and the higher Rockies. Likes grassy areas with rocks, but also chaparral and sagebrush. Differs from other western rattlesnakes by having *3 or more scales just across the nose between the nose openings.* Variable colors. Poisonous.

100. RED DIAMOND RATTLESNAKE, *Crotalus ruber.* 2½ to 5¼'. Found in southwest corner of California and south in Baja California. Likes rocky brushlands. *Usually has some reddish or pink in coloration;* lighter colored than Western Diamondback Rattlesnake. Poisonous.

101. WESTERN DIAMONDBACK RATTLESNAKE, *Crotalus atrox.* 2½ to 7½'. Found from southeastern California east through southern Arizona and New Mexico to most of Texas and Oklahoma, southeast corner of Kansas and northern Mexico. Likes brushy areas. *Contrasting black and white tail distinctive;* brown diamonds marked with small dark brown flecks or dots. Very aggressive and poisonous.

TURTLES

Order Testudinata—Turtles and Tortoises. (See also pages 72-73.)
Family Chelydridae—Musk, Mud and Snapping Turtles, etc.

102.   YELLOW MUD TURTLE, *Kinosternon flavescens.* 3 to 6" long.
Northwest corner and southeast of Arizona, east and north to Nebraska
and mid-Texas, and south into northern Mexico. Less mottling of head
and neck than in Sonora Mud Turtle (page 72). Can be fed raw meat and
fish.

Family Testudinidae—Fresh Water, Box and Marsh Turtles, etc.

103.   WESTERN BOX TURTLE, *Terrapene ornata.* 4 to 6". From
southeast Arizona northwest to southwest South Dakota, south to central
east Texas and south into Mexico. Likes short grass plains. *Distinctive radiating yellow bars on back shields.* Feeds on tender plant parts and insects.

104.   PAINTED TURTLE, *Chrysemys picta.* 4 to 10". Found from
Vancouver Island and north edge of central Oregon east to Minnesota and
eastern Wyoming, then south to eastern two-thirds of New Mexico and
north edge of Oklahoma. Likes shallow, quiet waters. *Back shields mar-
gined with yellow in front.* Feeds on water plants, insects, crayfish, frogs,
fish, etc.

105.   WESTERN POND TURTLE, *Clemmys marmorata.* 5 to 7". Found
from southeast British Columbia, southern Puget Sound area and west
coast of Oregon south in California west of mountains to Baja California;
small population around Reno, Nevada. *Distinctive networks of radiating
dashes on back plates.* Eats water plants, insects, and dead animals and
birds.

106.   POND SLIDER, *Chrysemys scripta.* 3 to 14½". Found from Texas, northeast Mexico, Oklahoma and south and east Kansas into the east.
Likes quiet waters with plants. *Has easily seen red or yellow blotch on side
of head; eye-like spots on plastron (under-side shields).* (Similar Southern
Terrapin is found in more eastern part of same area, but has no eye-spots
underneath, and usually has no red or yellow blotch on side of head.) Eats
water plants and animals.

Family Trionychidae—Softshelled Turtles.

107.   SPINY SOFTSHELL TURTLE, *Trionyx spiniferus.* 9 to 18½".
Found in lower Colorado River system, including the Gila River in Arizona; also in southeast Arizona, and central New Mexico, north Mexico; then
east from a line extending from central Montana through central Wyoming
and Colorado to southwest New Mexico. Likes large streams and rivers.
*The pancake shape, peculiar long nose and soft, leathery skin are very dis-
tinctive.* Molluscs, amphibians, fish, insects, crayfish are eaten; will eat raw
meat in captivity.

INTRODUCTION TO BLACK AND WHITE SECTION

The least colorful species of reptiles and amphibians are placed in this section of the book, described and with facing drawings. Remember that in each family there are usually some species also in the color plate section, and these should be looked at in order to compare them with the species from the same family placed here. Often shape of body, head, and limbs, as well as special arrangement of spots, blotches, lines and bars are as important to identification as is color and should be studied carefully. Study the descriptions carefully to see what things are most emphasized to help you make a proper identification. Proper arrangement of all species in their families and orders is given on pages 13 to 15.

AMPHIBIANS

Class Amphibia—Frogs, Toads and Salamanders. (See also pages 17-28.)
Order Caudata—Salamanders. (Lengths given are for adults.) These animals eat mainly insects and worms, and hide under surface objects and bark, but some are free swimming in fresh water.

LUNGLESS SALAMANDERS

Family Plethodontidae—Lungless Salamanders. (Breathe through skin.)

All western salamanders of this family live on land, but in damp places, usually under rocks, bark, boards, leaf-litter, etc. Most lay eggs in spring or summer, with hatching coming in late fall or winter when the rains begin.

108.   ENSATINA SALAMANDER, *Ensatina eschscholtzi*. 1½ to 3" long from nose to tail-base. This salamander has such distinctively different subspecies that the seven most important forms are pictured on page 51. It is found west of the crest of the Cascades, Sierras and southern California Mountains and outside of the great central Valley of California, generally in foothill localities. It likes the maple forests of Washington and Oregon, the redwood and douglas fir forests of northwestern California, the oak woodlands and chaparral of the warmer California foothills, and the yellow-pine and black oak forests of the middle slopes of the California mountains. Among western salamanders it can be immediately differentiated by the way *the tail is constricted at the base.* The colors are given below.

Subspecies *eschscholtzi.* Southern California coast. Reddish-orange above.
Subspecies *xanthoptica.* San Francisco Bay Region mainly. More orange than above subspecies. Iris of eye with large yellow patch.
Subspecies *oregonensis.* Western Washington, Oregon and northwest California. Brown or black above; iris of eye with small bright-colored patch.
Subspecies *picta.* Northwest corner of California; southwest corner of Oregon. Black above with yellowish or orange mottlings. Yellow patch in eye.
Subspecies *platensis.* Sierras. Dark brown above, with orange or red spots.
Subspecies *croceater.* Tehachapi Mountains. Black above with light spots.
Subspecies *klauberi.* Southern California mountains. Black above, with orange splotches.

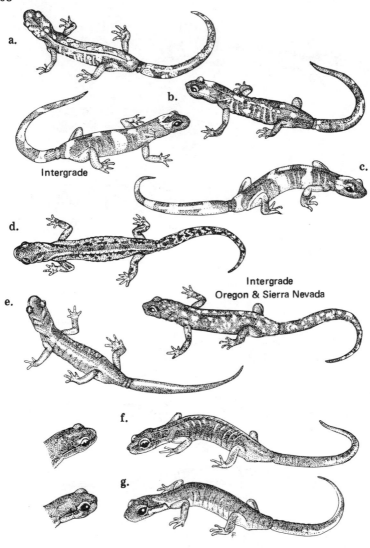

a. Sierra Nevada Salamander *(E. e. platensis)*

b. Yellow-blotched Salamander *(E. e. croceater)*

Intergrade

c. Large-blotched Salamander *(E. e. klauberi)*

d. Painted Salamander *(E. e. picta)*

Intergrade
Oregon & Sierra Nevada

e. Oregon Salamander *(E. e. oregonensis)*

f. Yellow-eyed Salamander *(E. e. xanthoptica)*

g. Monterey Salamander *(E. e. eschscholtzi)*

a. Sierra Nevada Salamander *(E. e. platensis)*
b. Yellow-blotched Salamander *(E. e. croceater)*
c. Large-blotched Salamander *(E. e. klauberi)*
d. Painted Salamander *(E. e. picta)*
e. Oregon Salamander *(E. e. oregonensis)*
f. Yellow-eyed Salamander *(E. e. xanthoptica)*
g. Monterey Salamander *(E. e. eschscholtzi)*

51

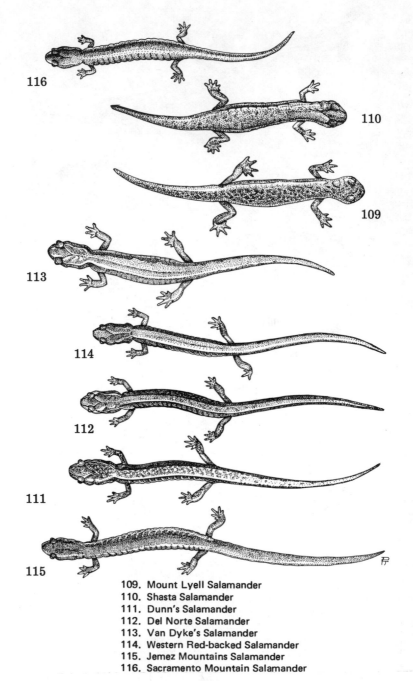

116

110

109

113

114

112

111

115

109. Mount Lyell Salamander
110. Shasta Salamander
111. Dunn's Salamander
112. Del Norte Salamander
113. Van Dyke's Salamander
114. Western Red-backed Salamander
115. Jemez Mountains Salamander
116. Sacramento Mountain Salamander

109.   MOUNT LYELL SALAMANDER, *Hydromantes platycephalus.*
1¾ to 2¾" from nose to tail-base. Found in high Sierras of California from
Sonora Pass to Sequoia National Park, generally underneath slabs of decom-
posing granite rock where there is some humus and water is seeping. Dark
brown to black above, but usually intermixed with patches and spots of
pale metallic yellow, gray or whitish; dark brown to blackish below, *usually
with broken white blotches that do not stretch across stomach or chest.*

110.   SHASTA SALAMANDER, *Hydromantes shastae.*   1¾ to 2½"
from nose to tail-base. Found in the mountains of Shasta County, California, from 1,000 to 2,500' altitude. Similar to above in appearance, but nose
longer and *white blotchings on undersides often extend completely across
chest or stomach.*

111.   DUNN'S SALAMANDER, *Plethodon dunni.* 2½ to 3" from nose
to tail-base.   Generally found among broken moss-covered rocks near
streams or in seepage areas in shade in western Oregon and southwestern
Washington.   Has dull greenish-yellow or olive-yellow to yellowish-brown
stripe down back, becoming blackish at tail tip; *dark-brownish to black
sides are lightly-spotted with white, yellowish or tan.*

112.   DEL NORTE SALAMANDER, *Plethodon elongatus.* 2½ to 2 7/8"
long from nose to tail-base. Found in humid coastal forest of northwestern corner of California and southwestern corner of Oregon, in moderately
damp soil under moss-covered broken rock. *Generally all black in adults,*
but young may have light brown to reddish-brown stripe down back; often
clouded, dark areas near middle of back. Slate gray on undersides.

113.   VAN DYKE'S SALAMANDER, *Plethodon vandykei.* 2 to 2½"
long from nose to tail-base. Found in damp or wet places under rocks be-
side streams, or in similar places where there is seepage; more rarely under
leaf litter or pieces of bark; in the mountains of western Washington and in
mountains around Lake Couer d'Alene in northern Idaho, usually near
Douglas Fir or maple trees. *A yellowish or light brown stripe, frequently
scalloped, extends down back and tail,* with most of upper parts black or
dark brown, but light flecks of white or gray on sides. Generally dark beneath, but with pale yellow throat. Most individuals in Idaho are dark below and on sides. Larch Mountain Salamander, *Plethodon larselli,* rare red
to orange bellied relative is found in dense firs of Columbia River Gorge.

114.   WESTERN RED-BACKED SALAMANDER, *Plethodon vehiculum*
2 to 2 3/8" long from nose to tail-base. Found under bark, logs, rocks, leaf-
litter, etc. in damp to very wet soil, in humid forests of northwestern Oregon north to southwestern British Columbia. Color varies from those with
well-defined reddish-brown to yellow back stripe to specimens almost completely black or those which are orange or yellow-splotched; bluish-black
on belly with numerous light-colored flecks and stipplings.

115.   JEMEZ MOUNTAINS SALAMANDER, *Plethodon neomexicanus.*
2 to 3" long from nose to tail-base. Found only in the Jemez Mountains
of Sandoval County, New Mexico. Very slim.

116.   SACRAMENTO MOUNTAIN SALAMANDER, *Aneides hardyi.* 2
to 2½" long from nose to tail-base. Found only in the Sacramento Mountains of N.M. at higher elevations. Blackish to brown with light markings.

53

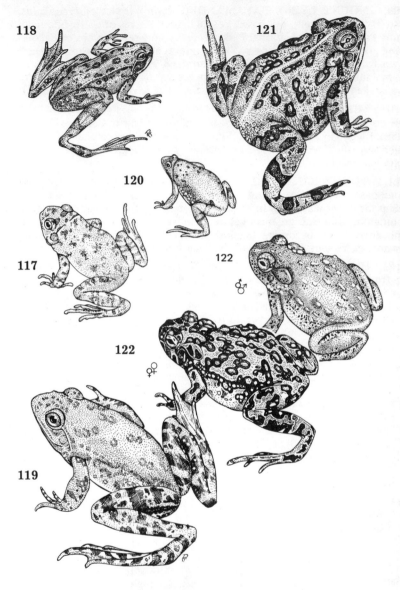

117. Barking Frog
118. Cascades Frog
119. Tarahumara Frog
120. Great Plains Narrow-mouthed Toad
121. Western Toad
122. Yosemite Toad

FROGS AND TOADS

Order Salientia—Frogs and Toads—Feed mainly on insects. (See also pages 21-28.)

Family Leptodactylidae—Barking Frogs.

117. BARKING FROG, *Eleutherodactylus augusti.* Adults up to 3" long. Found in crevices, caves or under rocks in wooded areas, especially in canyons, from southeastern Arizona and southwestern Texas down into Mexico. *The large broad head has a sharply-marked fold of skin just behind the ears;* the skin on the plain whitish belly often appears formed into a circular, central plate. Color purplish-gray to brown above, often suffused with light-yellowish and spotted or splotched with dark brown. Gives rapid "yap-yap" call, ending in bell-like ring.

Family Ranidae—Common Frogs. (See also pages 25-28.)

118. CASCADES FROG, *Rana cascadae.* Up to 2½" long. In Cascades and Olympic Mountains from Mt. Lassen to border of Canada. Similar to the Spotted Frog (see page 24), with strongly marked black spots on brownish back, but has a fainter light-colored stripe on the upper jaw, and is more sluggish in movements, trying to swim away from enemy rather than diving to bottom. It is generally yellowish below. Soft rasping chuckle.

119. TARAHUMARA FROG, *Rana tarahumarae.* Up to 4½" long in adults. Found from Pajarito Mountains of southeast Arizona south into Mexico; usually preferring springs and pools in canyons where there are oaks, walnuts, cottonwoods and pinyon pines. Throat usually dark, but not spotted; color above reddish-brown through grayish-olive to black-brown; legs banded and blotched with black; underneath yellow.

Family Microhylidae—Microhylids.

120. GREAT PLAINS NARROW-MOUTHED TOAD, *Gastrophryne olivacea.* ¾ to 1 3/8" long in adults. Found in southwestern Texas, also in southern Arizona and south in pools, along occasionally flowing streams and by springs; also under stones, logs and debris where dampness occurs. *The small head with pointed nose and the deep fold of skin back of the eye are distinctive as are the non-webbed fingers and toes.* Color above is light brown, brown or gray, sometimes with black spots. Buzzing call when nearby; sounds as sheep-like "baa-baa!" when far away.

Family Bufonidae—Common Toads. (See also pages 23-24.)

121. WESTERN TOAD, *Bufo boreas.* 2½ to 5". Found from Colorado and northern Rockies west to Pacific Coast, generally avoiding the dry deserts. Likes open valleys and meadows near streams, lakes and ponds, but also found less commonly in brushy areas and in woods. *Told from most other toads by absence of crests on top of head and by the whitish back stripe (rarely broken), and the light-colored warts set in middle of dark blotches.* Male gives low, tremulous, bird-like chirping.

122. YOSEMITE TOAD, *Bufo canorus.* 1¾ to 3" long in adults. Found in central and southern Sierras of California, mainly above 6,000 feet, in animal burrows and under rocks and logs in wet mountain meadows. Unlike the Western Toad, this toad has the *large paratoid glands on top of head separated by only a narrow width.* Females and young strikingly light and dark colored; male more uniform in color. Male gives rapid trilling call.

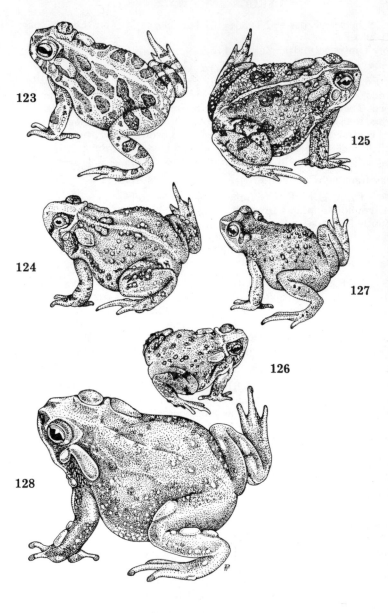

123. Great Plains Toad
124. Dakota Toad
125. Woodhouse's Toad
126. Southwestern Toad
127. Red-spotted Toad
128. Colorado River Toad

COMMON TOADS

123. GREAT PLAINS TOAD, *Bufo cognatus.* 2 to 4½" long in adults. Found in Great Plains grasslands, and in s.e. Utah, s.e. California, Arizona, New Mexico and Texas deserts, usually near or in irrigation ditches and pools, and rain pools; also found in underground burrows. Yellowish-brown to greenish or gray in color *with evenly spaced large dark (usually greenish) blotches on sides and back;* light brown to yellow underneath. The harsh, shrill voice vibrates like fast drum beats, but somewhat musical!

124. DAKOTA TOAD, *Bufo hemiophrys.* Up to 3¼" long in adults. Found from northwestern Minnesota, northeastern South Dakota and northeastern Montana north into Canada, generally near streams, ponds and lakes. *A bump with parallel sides appears on middle of head from nose to back of eyes;* colored above brownish or greenish with red bumps on back set in dark spots; white stripe down back. Mellow, trilling call lasts about three seconds, repeated about twice every minute.

125. WOODHOUSE'S TOAD, *Bufo woodhousei.* Up to 4¼" long in adults. Found from central and southern Great Plains to south central Washington, far eastern Oregon, southernmost Nevada and southeastern corner of California, in wooded river bottoms, canyons, deserts, etc., liking also marshes, irrigated lands and gardens. *Very prominent crests on top of head, and very long bumps or paratoid glands on back of neck.* Yellowish-brown or grayish with olive or green suffusion above; sometimes black or light brown; warts touched with reddish-brown or pink; white stripe down back. Trilling call sounds wheezy, or, at a distance, like "Waaaah" prolonged about two seconds.

126. SOUTHWESTERN TOAD, *Bufo microscaphus.* 2 to 3" long in adults. Found in southwestern California, west central, central and extreme northwestern Arizona; also in extreme southwestern Utah and in southeastern Nevada. Likes fairly dry canyons or washes where there are cottonwoods, willows or live oaks; also irrigated fields and ditches. Head with weak crests or none; colored variously greenish-gray, yellow, reddish or gray-brown above; rust-colored warts often appear in dark blotches; *light-colored V-shaped mark on head near eye;* plain whitish or yellowish below. Voice a long, clear trill with rise at beginning.

127. RED-SPOTTED TOAD, *Bufo punctatus.* Up to 3" long in adults. Found from central Texas and Oklahoma and southwestern Kansas west to southern Nevada and southeastern California and then south into Mexico, usually in canyons and deserts where there are water seepages or pools; also in irrigation and stock pools; from below sea level to over 6,000'. *Distance between eyes quite large;* usually pale grayish above, but may vary to light brownish; warts appear reddish or yellowish-brown in center of small dark patches; male has dark throat. Voice a clear, even-pitched liquid trill.

128. COLORADO RIVER TOAD, *Bufo alvarius.* Adults up to 6" long. Found from southeastern California and southern Arizona south, usually in or near permanent ponds and streams. *Large size, uniform dark color above (with few light-colored warts), and large warts on hind legs are distinctive.* Voice of male sounds like boat whistle.

57

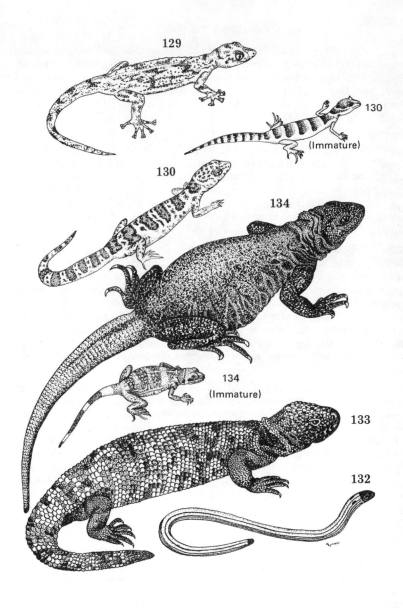

129. Leaf-toed Gecko
130. Banded Gecko
132. California Legless Lizard
133. Gila Monster
134. Chuckwalla

GECKOS, LEGLESS LIZARD, GILA MONSTER, CHUCKWALLA

Class Reptilia—Lizards, Snakes and Turtles. Body is covered with 4-sided scales, sometimes reinforced with horny plates (turtles). All are lung-breathers.

Order Squamata—Lizards and Snakes. (See also pages 27-48.)

Suborder Sauria—Lizards. Most have movable eyelids and legs, but a few (night lizards and Tuberculate Geckos) have non-movable eyelids, and the legless lizard no legs.

Family Gekkonidae—Geckos. Skin very soft. (Feed mainly at night on insects.)

129. LEAF-TOED GECKO, *Phyllodactylus xanti.* Up to 2¾" long from nose to tail-base in adults. Found from Palm Springs, California, south along western edge of Sonoran Desert and south into Baja California; likes rocky flats and hills, usually hiding in crevices by day. Body very flattened; *distinctive large plates are found on either side of claw on each toe* for aid in climbing; large eyes with vertical pupils (page 10) have no movable lids; pale brown, gray or light yellowish above, irregularly blotched, spotted and barred dark brown.

130. BANDED GECKO, *Coleonyx variegatus.* Up to 3" long from nose to tail-base in adults. Found in southern San Joaquin Valley, southwestern California and Mohave Desert, then east and south through southern Nevada to southeastern Arizona and northern Mexico, generally in rocky areas, but also in sand flats and washes. Hides by day under branches, trunks, boards, stones, dead animals, rock flakes, in crevices, etc. Has vertical pupils in eye and movable lids; colored above pinkish, yellowish or cream *with brown cross-bands* that are sometimes broken into spots; white below. Sometimes makes squeaking sound, and may run with tail curved over back.

131. TEXAS BANDED GECKO, *Coleonyx brevis.* (Not illustrated.) Very similar to above lizard, but found in central New Mexico, southwest Texas and south.

Family Anniellidae—Legless Lizards.

132. CALIFORNIA LEGLESS LIZARD, *Anniella pulchra.* 4½ to 6½" long in adults from nose to tail-base. Found from central California south, west of the Sierra crest, to Baja California, generally in localities where they can burrow in sand mixed with leaf mold or litter, but also in leaf mold and dirt under chaparral, up to about 6500' in Sequoia National Park. *Legless body, movable eyelid and breakable tail are distinctive.* Body above silvery-gray to brown-olive to black. Feeds mainly on insects and their larvae.

Family Helodermatidae—Venomous Lizards.

133. GILA MONSTER, *Heloderma suspectum.* 11 to 16" long from nose to tail-base in adults. Found from extreme southwest Utah and southeastern Nevada south through mainly desert areas of Arizona and southwest New Mexico into Texas and Mexico. *Large beaded scales;* distinctive spots, bars, irregular markings and dots of light brown, orange, orange-brown and blackish above; *tail with wide rings of dark and light colors;* yellowish-white below with brownish marks. *Poisonous.* Especially likes bird's eggs, also small lizards, birds and mammals.

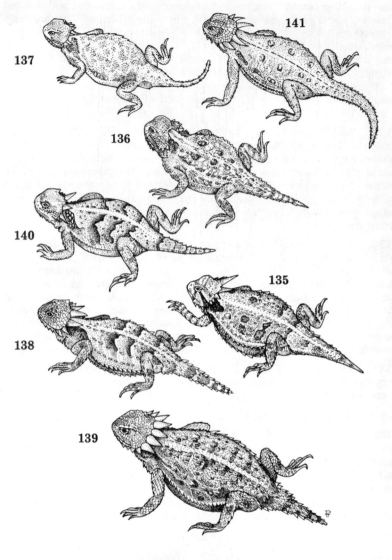

135. Texas Horned Lizard
136. Short-horned Lizard
137. Round-tailed Horned Lizard
138. Coast Horned Lizard
139. Regal Horned Lizard
140. Desert Horned Lizard
141. Flat-tailed Horned Lizard

Family Iquanidae—Iquanid Lizards.

134. CHUCKWALLA, *Sauromalus obesus.* 5 to 8"long from nose to tail-base in adults. Found in desert areas of southeastern California, southern Nevada, extreme southern Utah and western and southern Arizona, mainly on large rocks in flats and hills. *Fat body and loose folds of skin on sides* (except when lizard inflates body) are distinctive; males generally with black, some sometimes have light-flecked, fore-part of body and legs, with rest of body grayish or reddish; females mostly brown-gray or grayish, but with dark head and legs. Feeds on tender plant parts.

HORNED LIZARDS

135. TEXAS HORNED LIZARD,*Phrynosoma cornutum.* 2 to 4" long from nose to tail-base in adults. Found from Kansas and Oklahoma south and west through Texas, southeast Colorado, eastern and southern New Mexico to southeast Arizona and northeast Mexico, mainly in open flat country with brush, but also in rocky areas and hardpan dry river and stream bottoms. Has two fringes of sharp scales along sides, *two very long pointed horns on back of neck*, and a few large pointed scales at top edge of throat. Gray-brown through yellowish and reddish-brown or tan to gray above, with dark blotches, particularly *a large dark brown to blackish blotch on each side of neck behind head.* Most horned lizards run about on surface of ground in daylight hunting for insects and spiders.

136. SHORT-HORNED LIZARD, *Phrynosoma douglassi.* 2 to 3¾" long from nose to tail-base in adults. Found in scattered areas of theWest, east of the Cascades and Sierras from eastern Oregon and Washington to the Great Plains and Mexico, generally avoiding the highest mountains and hotter deserts (except in Texas and New Mexico). Likes semiarid flats in brushy country, but also found on the short-grass plains and in the pine-spruce and pinyon-juniper forests. *The short head spines and small chin shields (page 11) are distinctive;* a single row of spines on the side. Color gray, through brown, yellow-brown, reddish or yellowish above, with rows of dark blotches or bars on back, edged behind with white or pale yellow.

137. ROUND-TAILED HORNED LIZARD, *Phrynosoma modestum.* Up to 2 7/8" long in adults from nose to tail-base. Found from central New Mexico, southeast Arizona and west Texas south, in arid, brushy areas. *No fringe scales on side; tail quite slender and round,* becoming wide suddenly at base; light-colored above, but with dark blotch on each side of neck, and either side of tail near base.

138. COAST HORNED LIZARD, *Phrynosoma coronatum.* 3 to 4¼" long from nose to tail-base in adults. Found from central Sacramento Valley and San Francisco Bay Area south, always west of the mountains, to Baja California. *Two distinctive long horns at middle back of head;* 2 rows of spines fringe side; 2 or 3 rows of pointed scales at side of throat. Colorful gray, brown, yellowish or reddish mottled above, with black blotches on back, largest near head. May shoot blood from eye to bluff enemy.

139. REGAL HORNED LIZARD,*Phrynosoma solare.* 3 to 4 5/8" long from nose to tail-base in adults. Found in central and south-central Arizona and south into Mexico, in arid areas, usually associated with mesquite and saguaro cacti. *Four crowded together long horns at back of head,* single row of ringed scales on side; pale gray to yellow-brown or reddish above, with dark blotches along sides and back.

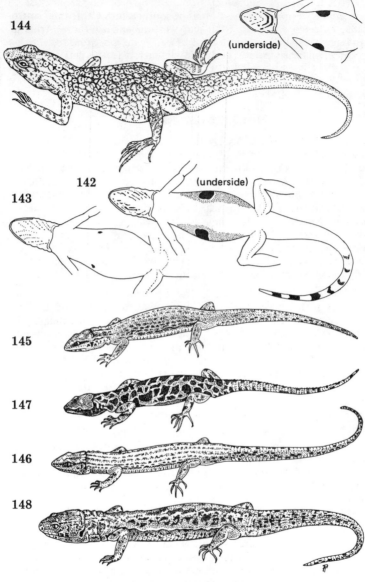

142. Colorado Desert Fringe-toed Lizard
143. Coachella Valley Fringe-toed Lizard
144. Mohave Fringe-toed Lizard
145. Desert Night Lizard
146. Arizona Night Lizard
147. Granite Night Lizard
148. Island Night Lizard

140. DESERT HORNED LIZARD, *Phrynosoma platyrhinos.* 2 5/8 to 3¾" long from nose to tail-base. Found in deserts from southeast Oregon and southwest Idaho south through Nevada and western Utah to southeast California, western Arizona and extreme northwest Mexico, associated mostly with sand and gravel soils. *Two comparatively short large horns at rear of head;* 1 row of fringe scales on side; grayish above with dark markings.

141. FLAT-TAILED HORNED LIZARD, *Phrynosoma m'calli.* 2¾ to 3 3/8" from nose to tail-base in adults. Found in southeastern California and extreme southwestern corner of Arizona, and south, associated with hummocks topped by creosote bushes, burro-weed and similar bushes. *Tail quite flat and head spines longer and more narrow than in other species;* 2 rows of side scales; *distinctive thin black line down gray back.*

SAND AND NIGHT LIZARDS

142. COLORADO DESERT FRINGE-TOED LIZARD, *Uma notata.* 3 to 4½" from head to tail-base in adults. Found from the Salton Sea in southeastern California south and east into extreme southeast Arizona and on into Mexico, living in wind-blown sand. Most sand lizards look alike on upper surface with *dark markings on gray-white upper surface* (as shown in picture on page 62), but appear different beneath as also shown. They may be seen running over sand-dunes and then diving into the loose sand where they burrow or "swim" beneath the surface to hide from potential enemies. This species has a *strongly-marked throat, but the black crescents are absent or faint in middle of throat.* Sand lizards feed mainly on insects.

143. COACHELLA VALLEY FRINGE-TOED LIZARD, *Uma inornata.* 3 to 4½" from head to tail-base. Found in the Coachella Valley of southern California and the nearby San Gorgonio Pass. Similar to above lizard, but with *tiny (or absent) dark spots on side of belly, and without black crescents on throat.*

144. MOJAVE FRINGE-TOED LIZARD, *Uma scoparia.* Similar to above two lizards, but found almost solely in Mohave Desert. Has *very sharp black crescents in middle of throat.*

Family Xantusiidae—Night Lizards. Very soft, granular skin; no movable eyelids; pupils of eyes vertical to help in night sight (see page 10).

145. DESERT NIGHT LIZARD, *Xantusia vigilis.* 1½ to 1 7/8" from nose to base of tail. Found mainly in Mohave Desert, also in s.e. Utah, so. California coast range and south into Mexico; almost always associated with yucca plants, particularly the Joshua Tree. Hides mainly under trunks and in leaves of dead yuccas, but also in leaves of live yuccas, and in nearby rock crevices. *Stomach plates form 12 longitudinal rows down mid-body.* Gray, yellowish, olive or brownish above, covered with dark dots or spots; whitish to dull gray or greenish-yellow below. More active in daytime than most night lizards. Night lizards feed mainly on insects.

146. ARIZONA NIGHT LIZARD, *Xantusia arizonae.* 1¾ to 2½" from nose to tail-base. Found in a narrow area along the southern edge of the Colorado River Plateau in central Arizona, usually associated with granite boulders and chaparral or brush. *Stomach plates, as in Yucca Night Lizard, form 12 longitudinal rows down mid-body.* Olive-yellow above with grayish suffusion and marked by irregular longitudinal rows of dark spots.

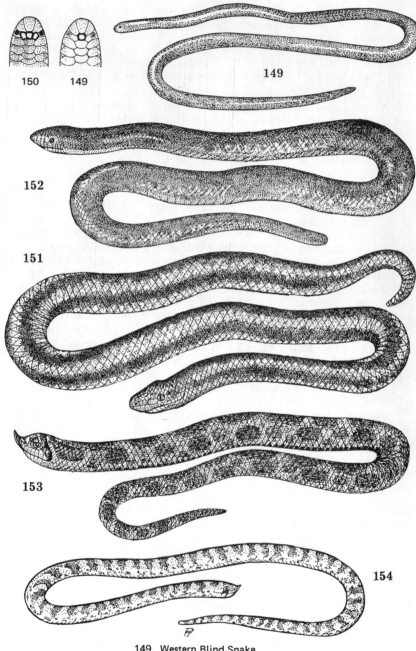

149. Western Blind Snake
150. Texas Blind Snake
151. Rosy Boa
152. Rubber Boa
153. Western Hognose Snake
154. Western Hook-nosed Snake

147.   GRANITE NIGHT LIZARD, *Xantusia henshawi.* 2 to 2 7/8"
from nose to tail-base in adults. Found from San Bernardino County, California south in hilly and mountainous country, usually associated with large granite rocks where it hides in cracks and under rock flakes. *Stomach plates form 14 longitudinal rows down mid-body; body very flattened.* Color above yellow, but covered with large brownish-black spots; tail more banded-looking than other night lizards.

148.   ISLAND NIGHT LIZARD, *Klauberina riversiana.* Length is 2½ to 3¾" from nose to base of tail in adults. Found only on San Clemente, Santa Barbara and San Nicholas Islands off the southern California coast. *Much larger and more irregularly blotched than other night lizards.*

WORM SNAKES, BOAS, AND COMMON SNAKES

Suborder Serpentes—Snakes. Eyelids not movable; no legs. (See also pages 38-48.)

Family Leptotyphlopidae—Blind (or Worm) Snakes. No apparent neck.

149.   WESTERN BLIND SNAKE, *Leptotyphlops humilis.* Adults about 9 to 12" long, and less than ¼" in diameter. Found from southern Californian coast and Mohave Desert south and east to the southern edge of New Mexico and southwest Texas and down into Mexico, generally in sandy and rocky deserts or in brush-covered and rock-covered hillsides where they burrow in the loose sandy soil. *Worm-like shape is distinctive;* color pinkish to light brown; *scales on side of face one less in number than in Texas Blind Snake.* Feeds mainly on ants and termites.

150.   TEXAS BLIND SNAKE, *Leptotyphlops dulcis.* Similar in size to Western Blind Snake. Found from Oklahoma south and west through much of Texas, the east and southern edge of New Mexico, to the extreme southeast corner of Arizona and northeast Mexico. *Similar to Western Blind Snake, but has one more scale on side of face.*

Family Boidae—Boas. Remnants of legs appear as spurs on sides of body near base of tail; pupils of eyes vertical for night seeing. Feed mainly on small mammals, lizards and birds, killing by strangulation.

151.   ROSY BOA, *Lichanura trivirgata.* Adults usually 2 to 3' long. Found from Mohave Desert and southern California coast south and west into southwestern Arizona and northwestern Mexico with exception of area around Salton Sea and immediately south and southeast. The subspecies *gracia* in the east of its range lives in brush-covered deserts and rocky canyons or nearby mountains. The subspecies *roseofusca* lives in brushy and rock-covered hillsides of the California coast. *No enlarged scales between eyes;* colored dark gray, bluish or brown-gray above, with *3 long, broad, reddish-brown stripes down back;* yellowish-white below.

152.   RUBBER BOA, *Charina bottae.* Adults 13 to 29" long. Found in mountainous and humid areas of the west from western Wyoming and northern Utah to central western Washington and the southern California mountains, but generally avoiding very humid coastal areas of Washington and Oregon, preferring coniferous forests. *A large plate appears on head between eyes; tail blunt;* color yellow-brown to dark brown, often tinged with yellow, green or blue. Burrows by day in loose soil or leaf litter, coming out at night to hunt salamanders, lizards, mice, etc.

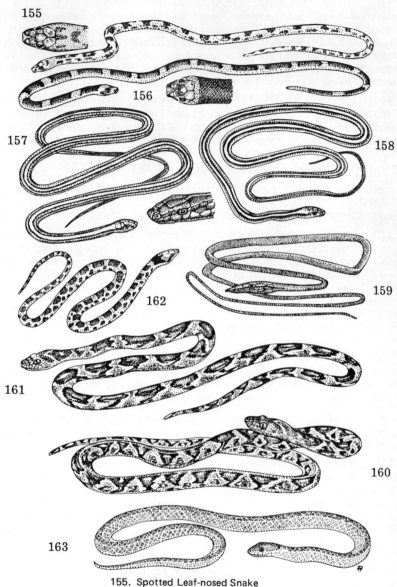

155. Spotted Leaf-nosed Snake
156. Saddled Leaf-nosed Snake
157. Western Patch-nosed Snake
158. Mountain Patch-nosed Snake
159. Vine Snake
160. California Lyre Snake
161. Sonora Lyre Snake
162. Spotted Night Snake
163. Western Ground Snake

Family Colubridae—Common Snakes. Large and regular head plates.

153. WESTERN HOGNOSE SNAKE, *Heterodon nasicus.* Adults around 16 to 32" long. Found in Great Plains and in a curve into southeastern Arizona and northern Mexico, living in sandy or gravelly soil among grasses and bushes. Scale on nose much-enlarged, spade-shaped and upturned; tail with spine at tip. Color pale brown to olive-gray or yellowish above, with olive-brown or black-brown blotches down back. Often mistaken for rattlesnake, but neck not narrow. Burrows in loose soil, hunting worms and insects. May play dead or puff up head and hiss ferociously.

154. WESTERN HOOK-NOSED SNAKE, *Ficimia cana.* 8 to 13" long in adults. Found from southeastern Arizona to southwestern Texas and south, mainly in open areas. *Scale on nose hooked up and pointed.* Color grayish-brown or yellow with dark-brown bars.

155. SPOTTED LEAF-NOSED SNAKE, *Phyllorhynchus decurtatus.* 12 to 20" long in adults. Found in Mohave and Sonoran Deserts from southern Nevada and southeastern California through west and south Arizona to Mexico, usually in sandy and rocky places with some brush around. Color light yellow-brown, pinkish, gray-brown or even whitish above, *with a row of 17 or more dark blotches down the middle of the back;* 1 to 3 rows of smaller blotches along sides; *a leaf-like saddle on nose.* Active at night, eating small lizards and their eggs.

156. SADDLED LEAF-NOSED SNAKE, *Phyllorhynchus browni.* Same size as above. Found in south central Arizona and south into Mexico, in brushy areas, particularly mesquite and saltbush; sometimes found under stones and on black-top highways. Similar to above, but *with less than 17 dark blotches in row down middle of back.*

157. WESTERN PATCH-NOSED SNAKE, *Salvadora hexalepis.* 2 to 4' long in adults. Found from west central Nevada east of the Sierras and south in mainly brushy desert areas to southeast Utah, southern California, western and southern Arizona, southwestern New Mexico, and extreme southwestern Texas, into Mexico. *The rear pair of chin shields (page 12) under the mouth are separated by 2 or 3 smaller scales;* light gray or grayish-brown above, with 2 dark stripes down back; a few may have only one broad dark back stripe. Active by day, catching lizards and small mammals.

158. MOUNTAIN PATCH-NOSED SNAKE, *Salvadora grahamiae.* From southeastern Arizona, most of New Mexico, to southwestern Texas, mainly in forested mountains. Similar to above snake, but with none or 1 scale between rear pair of chin shields (page 12).

159. VINE SNAKE, *Oxybelis aeneus.* 3 to 4' long. From southeastern Arizona south, in brush and oak-covered hills and canyons. *Extreme thinness and peculiar spear-shaped head are distinctive.* Pale gray above, changing to light yellow-brown in front part of body. Active in daytime catching lizards. Slightly poisonous.

160. CALIFORNIA LYRE SNAKE, *Trimorphodon vandenburghi.* 2 to 3½' long. Found on southern California coast and east to edge of desert, mostly among rocks where it stays in crevices during the day. *A slim snake with a comparatively broad head; single or divided anal plate;* dark brown blotches on light brown or gray back; *V-shaped mark on head.* Feeds mainly on lizards and mammals. Slightly poisonous, but harmless to man.

67

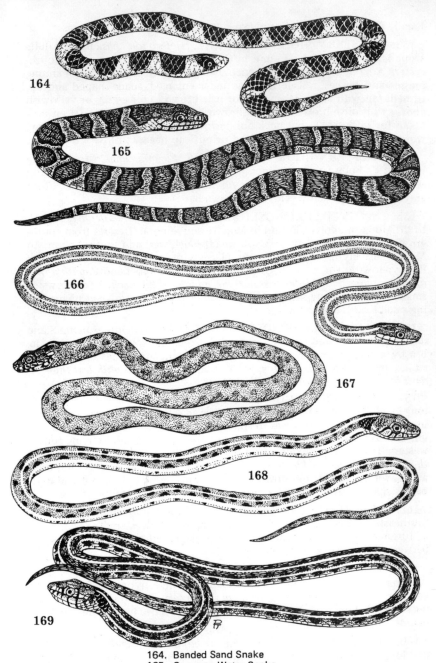

164. Banded Sand Snake
165. Common Water Snake
166. Western Ribbon Snake
167. Narrow-headed Garter Snake
168. Black-necked Garter Snake
169. Mexican Garter Snake

161. SONORA LYRE SNAKE, *Trimorphodon lambda.* Similar to 160, but found in southeast California, southern Nevada and in Arizona.

162. SPOTTED NIGHT SNAKE, *Hypsiglena torquata.* 12 to 19" long. Found in drier parts of West from eastern Washington, California great Central Valley, and southern Kansas south and west to Mexico, in many habitats in the West. *The smooth black scales and vertical pupil in the eye (page 12) separate it from garter and glossy snakes.* Gray, yellowish or yellow gray-brown above, with numerous brown spots forming a pattern; *large dark blotches on side of neck; 2 anal plates (page 12).* Feeds by night on lizards, toads and salamanders. Slightly poisonous, but not dangerous.

163. WESTERN GROUND SNAKE, *Sonora semiannulata.* 9 to 12" long. Found from southeast Oregon and southwest Idaho south through Nevada and east edge of California, southeast Utah and western and southern Arizona to southern New Mexico and northern Mexico in sandy areas. Similar to shovel-nosed snakes (page 43), but has more rounded nose; may be marked above either with dark cross-bands on brownish-gray back, or with sharply-marked back stripe of red or rusty or pink. Feeds on insects.

SAND, WATER AND GARTER SNAKES

164. BANDED SAND SNAKE, *Chilomeniscus cinctus.* 9 to 11" long in adults. Found in the southeast tip of California, southern Arizona and northwestern Mexico. This is a highly specialized snake, *adapted by smooth scales, shovel-shaped mouth and strong, thick neck for burrowing in sand.* Many dark cross-bands show against yellowish, whitish or orange-red ground color. Feeds mainly on insects, spiders and centipedes.

165. COMMON WATER SNAKE, *Natrix sipedon.* 2 to 4' long in adults. Found from eastern Colorado, Nebraska, Kansas, southern South Dakota and eastern Texas east, in or near lakes, ponds, streams, marshes and rivers. *Body thicker than garter snakes, and has two anal plates (page 12);* scales keeled (page 12). The light to dark gray, light brown or brown back is crossed by wide dark reddish-brown or dark gray cross-bands in front half, changing to squares in back. Likes fish and tadpoles especially, but also crayfish, frogs, toads and salamanders and, more rarely, mice and shrews.

Garter Snakes—Back plates are keeled; single anal plate (page 12).

166. WESTERN RIBBON SNAKE, *Thamnophis proximus.* (A garter snake.) 2 to 2½' long in adults. Found from east edge of New Mexico through most of Texas and Kansas east, mainly near or in swamps, lakes, ponds and streams, liking thick vegetations near water. *Tail usually much more than ¼ of total length; upper lip scales plain light-colored,* contrasting with the darker olive, brown, dark gray or black of upper surface, which has 3 light-colored stripes down back. Feeds on amphibians and small fish.

167. NARROW-HEADED GARTER SNAKE, *Thamnophis rufipunctatus.* 1¾ to 3' long in adults. Found in Arizona and New Mexico mainly along southern edge of Colorado River Plateau; also in north central Mexico, preferring open cottonwood or oak woods near water, generally in rocky canyons. Usually has 8 upper lip scales; rarely has back striped, but *appears brownish to olive-gray above, with many brownish-black spots;* olive-brown on head. Feeds on amphibians and small fish.

170. Mohave Rattlesnake
171. Black-tailed Rattlesnake
172. Speckled Rattlesnake
173. Ridge-nosed Rattlesnake
174. Tiger Rattlesnake
175. Rock Rattlesnake
176. Sidewinder

168.   BLACK-NECKED GARTER SNAKE, *Thamnophis dorsalis.* 1 to 2' long in adults. Found from southeastern Utah, southeast Colorado, most of New Mexico and eastern Arizona south, through southwestern Texas into Mexico, preferring mountain springs, streams and seepages, often where walnut trees and oaks are found. *Very large black blotches on neck are distinctive;* light stripe down middle of back, with 2 checkered rows of square black blotches on brownish-yellow, brown or olive back and sides, fading out in last third of length. Feeds mainly on amphibians.

169.   MEXICAN GARTER SNAKE, *Thamnophis eques.* 1¾ to 3¼' long in adults. Found from central and southeastern Arizona and southwestern New Mexico south into Mexican highlands, mainly in or near water. *Distinctive small dark spots appear in alternating rows against olive or brown background color* and between center and sides are yellowish or light colored stripes; *black neck blotches and light-colored crescents near corners of mouth are also distinctive.* Looks like the Checkered Garter Snake (page 42), and the Black-necked Garter Snake (above), but has its side stripe that is on the front of the body on both the 3rd and 4th scale rows up from the belly, not just on the 3rd. Lives mostly on frogs.

RATTLESNAKES

Family Crotalidae—Pit Vipers, including Rattlesnakes, Copperheads and Mocassins. A heat-sensing pit appears in front of nostril; arrow-head-shaped head; poison fangs in front of mouth are hinged; rattlesnakes have rattles. Feed mainly on mammals, such as mice, rabbits and squirrels, but some also eat lizards and birds. (See also pages 45-46.) Poisonous.

170.   MOJAVE RATTLESNAKE, *Crotalus scutulatus.* 2 to 4' long in adults. Found from Mohave Desert in Nevada and California south through western and southern Arizona and extreme southeastern New Mexico and southwestern Texas into Mexican highlands. Prefers bushy desert, rarely below 2000 feet. *Distinctive 2 large scales between the even larger scales just above eyes on head; usually has light stripe from eye back to above corner of mouth;* general color green through gray, olive green and yellowish to greenish-brown, with dark-brown diamonds, lighter in back. Poisonous.

171.   BLACK-TAILED RATTLESNAKE, *Crotalus molossus.* 2½ to 4½' long in adults. Found mainly in low mountains from north-central Arizona, central New Mexico and southwest Texas south into Mexican highlands, preferring brushy hills and rock-slides. Easily told from other rattlesnakes by black tail and nose; mostly colored yellow, brownish-olive, grayish or greenish above, with dark brown, olive-brown or black cross-bands or jagged diamonds, edged with white and with light central markings. Poisonous.

172.   SPECKLED RATTLESNAKE, *Crotalus mitchelli.* 2 to 4½' in adults. Found from Mohave and Sonoran Deserts of southern Nevada, western Arizona and southern California west to the coast in San Diego County and south into northwest Mexico, usually in rocky areas of hills and low mountains, but sometimes in sandy flats. *Told best by the way the dark reddish to brown or black dots on the back are formed into groups of variously-shaped splotches.* Color of upper parts very variable, from yellow-white through light gray to pink, light brown and brown. Mainly a night hunter of small mammals, birds and lizards. Poisonous.

178

177

179

177. Snapping Turtle
178. Sonora Mud Turtle
179. Desert Tortoise

173.   RIDGE-NOSED RATTLESNAKE, *Crotalus willardi.*   1½ to 2' long.   Found in the Huachuca and Santa Rita Mountains of southern Arizona and southward, mainly above 5500' in forested canyons and ridges. There is *a ridge on each side of nose; widely-spaced brown blotches on back have pale long centers;* light line along side of face and nose; top of head black-dotted.   Feeds, mainly in daylight.

174.   TIGER RATTLESNAKE, *Crotalus tigris.*   2 to 3' long in adults. Found in central and south-central Arizona and south into Sonora, Mexico, in rocky foothills and canyons of desert mountains.   *Usually more sharply cross-banded than other rattlesnakes in the West,* though bands sometimes have vague edges.   Blotches and bands on back are dark brown or dark gray, against gray, bluish-gray, lavender, light brown, etc.

175.   ROCK RATTLESNAKE, *Crotalus lepidus.*   1 1/3 to 2¼' long in adults.   Found from southeast Arizona, southwest New Mexico and southwest Texas south into the Mexican highlands, in mountain rocky situations with trees widely spaced.   Gray, bluish-gray or greenish-gray in color, with dark brown or black cross-bands on back (more diffuse in eastern subspecies); young snakes sometimes have brilliant yellow color on tails.

176.   SIDEWINDER, *Crotalus cerastes.*   1½ to 2½' in adults.   Found in Mohave and Sonoran Deserts of Nevada, southeastern Utah, California, Arizona and Mexico, generally where some sand is present and favorable for its peculiar sidewinding motion.   *Horn-like knobs over the eyes are distinctive as is its light sandy coloration.*   Nocturnal.

TURTLES AND TORTOISES

Order Testudinata—Turtles and Tortoises.   (See also pages 47-49.)
Family Chelydridae—Snapping Turtles, Musk and Mud Turtles, etc.

177.   SNAPPING TURTLE, *Chelydra serpentina.*   9 to 15" in adults. Found in the Great Plains and east from Saskatchewan and Montana south to eastern New Mexico, Texas and Mexico, in quiet or sluggish ponds or streams.   *Distinctive powerful jaws, long armored tail and 3 ridges on shell.* Usually dull brown or black above, whitish or yellowish below.   Omnivorous feeder on small animals and plants.   Snaps ferociously.   Catches ducks.

178.   SONORA MUD TURTLE, *Kinosternon sonoriense.*   Closely resembles the Yellow Mud Turtle (see page 47).   4 to 7" in adults.   Found along the lower Colorado River in California and Arizona, also in central and southeastern Arizona and southwestern New Mexico, and southwest Texas and Mexico, in springs, rivers, ponds, creeks, etc.   Carapace (shell) rather smooth and non-flaring; plastron shields of underside in five pairs, plus an unpaired throat shield; olive-colored above, with scattered dark lines and spots; head and neck mottled and flecked with light and dark areas.   Eats molluscs, insects, snails, salamanders, etc.

Family Testudinidae—Land Tortoises, Marsh and Freshwater Turtles, etc.

179.   DESERT TORTOISE, *Gopherus agassizi.*   10 to 14" in adults. Found in desert areas from southern Nevada, southwestern Utah and southeastern California through western and southern Arizona into Sonora, Mexico.   Distinctive high carapace with squarish shields showing growth rings; shields brownish with yellowish centers, or sometimes dark brown all over. Burrows in ground in heat or cold; feeds mainly on grasses and herbs.   Rare.

SUGGESTED REFERENCES

The following books are useful guides to a deeper knowledge of reptiles and amphibians.

Bellairs, Angus. *Life of Reptiles.* 2 volumes, (Natural History Series), Universe, New York, N.Y., 10016. 1970.

Breen, J.F. *Encyclopedia of Reptiles and Amphibians.* T.F.H. Publications, Neptune City, N.J., 07753. 1970.

Cochran, Doris M. *Living Amphibians of the World.* Doubleday, Garden City, N.Y., 11530. 1961.

Cochran, Doris M., and Goin, Coleman J. *New Field Book of Reptiles and Amphibians.* Putnam, New York, N.Y., 10016. 1970.

Conant, Roger. *Field Guide to Reptiles and Amphibians of Eastern North America.* Houghton Mifflin, Boston, Mass., 02108. 1958.

Cope, E.D. *Batrachia of North America.* Lundberg, Augusta, West Virginia, 26704. 1963.

Ditmars, Raymond. *Reptiles of the World,* Revised Edition. Macmillan, New York, N.Y. 10022. 1966.

Gans, Carl (editor). *Biology of the Reptilia.* 3 volumes, Academy Press, Campbell, CA. 95008. 1969-1970.

Inger, Robert F. and Schmidt, Karl P. *Living Reptiles of the World.* Doubleday, Garden City, N.Y. 11530. 1957.

Kingsley, Noble. *Biology of the Amphibia.* Peter Smith, Goucester, MA. 01930.

Leviton, Alan. *Amphibians and Reptiles of North America.* Doubleday, Garden City, N.Y., 11530. 1972.

Smyth, H. Rucker. *Amphibians and Their Ways.* Macmillan, New York, N.Y. 10022. 1962.

Stebbins, Robert C. *Field Guide to the Western Reptiles and Amphibians.* Houghton Mifflin, Boston, Mass. 02108. 1966.

INDEX OF COMMON NAMES

The numbers in italic represent the pages where the illustrations may be found.

COMMON NAMES

COMMON NAMES

INDEX OF SCIENTIFIC NAMES

SCIENTIFIC INDEX